BRENTWOOD

Praise for <u>Why Buffalo Dance</u>

"In *Why Buffalo Dance* Susan Chernak McElroy takes us on a journey through the seasons of our lives as a courageous, loving, and skilled guide in the art of living. She reveals once again her extraordinary gift of being an ever-attentive, wise, and compassionate witness to the cycles of life, while showing us how to gaze deeply into the mirror of nature to find the pulse, pace, and rhythm of our own life waiting to be lived."

— Michael Brant DeMaria, PhD, psychologist, wilderness guide, and author of *Ever Flowing On*

"I have known Susan for many years and always refer to her previous wise and meaningful books when I lecture. Since I am in love with her and her writing, you may question the validity of my comment, but let me assure you I am sincere in what I say. *Why Buffalo Dance* has helped turn my life into a poem. It is an incredible pleasure to read, and I find it hard to compare the feeling it gives me to any other experience except love. It has helped me to fall in love with life again despite all the difficulties we all experience on a daily basis. I often advise people that when they awaken in the morning, they should act as if they are extraterrestrials visiting Earth for the first time so they will become aware of the beauty that surrounds them, rather than be annoyed by the weather, sounds that kept them awake, or other bits of meaningless nonsense. Susan, through her life, words, and wounds, shows me I am capable of enjoying life and becoming aware, too. As Thornton Wilder wrote, 'In love's service only the wounded soldier can serve.' Susan, bless you for your gift of love, life, and healing."

— Dr. Bernie S. Siegel, author of
365 Prescriptions for the Soul and *101 Exercises for the Soul*

"*Why Buffalo Dance* is much more than just another book of meditations. It is a collection of wisdom inspired by the purest teachers of truth, our nonhuman relatives of the wild. Filtered through Susan McElroy's unique and delightful perspective on life, this collection of meditations is truly meaningful to those who would live a richer experience, one that comes from a better understanding of who we are in the great circle of life. As I read through its chapters, I found myself saying 'Ahh, now it all makes sense!' Susan has compiled wisdoms often ignored in this modern world, wisdoms that when applied, bring refreshing new life into one's walk on Earth."

— James Medicine Tree, author of
The Way of the Sacred Pipe

WHY BUFFALO
DANCE

Also by Susan Chernak McElroy

All My Relations

Animals as Guides for the Soul

Animals as Teachers and Healers

Heart in the Wild

WHY BUFFALO
DANCE

ANIMAL AND WILDERNESS
MEDITATIONS THROUGH THE SEASONS

SUSAN CHERNAK McELROY

ILLUSTRATIONS BY TRACY PITTS

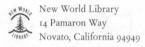

New World Library
14 Pamaron Way
Novato, California 94949

Illustrations by Tracy Pitts
Text design and typography by Tona Pearce Myers

Library of Congress Cataloging-in-Publication Data
McElroy, Susan Chernak
  Why buffalo dance : animal and wilderness meditations through the seasons
/ Susan Chernak McElroy.
     p.   cm.
ISBN-13: 978-1-57731-542-1 (hardcover : alk. paper)
1. Seasons—Religious aspects—Meditations. 2. Nature—Religious
aspects—Meditations. 3. Animals—Religious aspects—Meditations. I. Title.
BL590.M43 2006
204'.32—dc22   2006013988

First printing, October 2006
ISBN-10: 1-57731-542-1
ISBN-13: 978-1-57731-542-1
Printed in Canada on acid-free, partially recycled paper
Distributed by Publishers Group West

For Teresa —
Thank you for your grace and your wisdom,
and for your company on the journey.
No woman could ask for a finer sister.

CONTENTS

Summer

Autumn

FOREWORD

I MAY NOT BE THE BEST person to write about *Why Buffalo Dance* because I don't consider myself a very spiritual person, and this is a very spiritual book. However, I found myself drawn into the stories Susan Chernak McElroy tells, and the images and animals have stayed with me.

Worth the price of this book is the enchanting story of Strongheart and the large buck, who suddenly realized there was no reason to be predator and prey; they could be just two beings on this earth. Susan delicately relates this lesson to her reprieve from cancer. She learns from every being she meets in every season, and so do we.

She fosters animals at every opportunity, and these stories are truly awe-inspiring. For example, who would ever have expected a newborn fawn to make it after she was literally dropped by her mother as her mother ran away in fear? But make it she does, thanks to Susan's complete dedication. Susan has a passion to save at whatever cost to her own comfort, as in the case of the magpie who did not appear to have any chance of survival. Most of us would have simply walked away, but not Susan, who reminds us that he's not just "a" magpie; he's "this" magpie. And she is not simply "a" human; she's "this" human, who will feel wretched if she leaves him to die on his own.

Her reward is great: who would not be thrilled to have a magpie accompany her on long walks in the forest? The bird rode on Susan's shoulder and flew from tree to tree alongside her. And he taught her the lesson that all of us seem to need to learn from animals: he brought fullness and presence to all tasks, making all work dignified and all play noble and important.

These are just some of the many lessons Susan learns from the animals and then imparts to us. At age sixty-five, now that I have learned these lessons from Susan, I keep them in mind as I play with my nine-year-old and four-year-old sons. Her stories are deeply enriching.

— Jeffrey Moussaieff Masson, PhD, author of
When Elephants Weep

INTRODUCTION

The power of the world always works in circles, and everything tries to be round....Even the seasons form a great circle in their changing, and always come back again to where they were. The life of a man is a circle from childhood to childhood, and so it is in everything where power moves.

— BLACK ELK, *BLACK ELK SPEAKS*

EVER SINCE I MOVED TO A LANDSCAPE with four distinct seasons, I have dreamed of creating a book where animals and nature speak simply to us about the power and mystery of the seasons. Because no matter what our perceived differences, we all — animals, plants, and elements — share the cycles of the year and are affected deeply by the turning of the world. In this time of great

distance between ourselves and wild nature, the primal lessons of how to live harmoniously with our inner and outer cycles are needed perhaps more than ever before.

In this small guidebook, I've gathered the voices of animals, elements, and land into a collection of meditations exploring the seasons of nature and the seasons of our lives. The stories are built upon the foundation of a few simple assumptions about nature and our relationship to her. While the basics of these meditations are ancient, the creatures who stalk these pages will teach you new truths about life and living, in a way that is uniquely, fascinatingly, and honorably their own.

Nature: The First Revelation

These stories are grounded in a vision of nature as the first revelation. I so wish this idea had been mine, but I discovered it most eloquently unfolded in the writings of Brother Wayne Teasdale, a modern-day monk and mystic. In *Mystic Heart*, Teasdale writes, "Natural mysticism is the primordial revelation.... Long before writing and tradition, the divine reality communicated its light to us through all that is. Every ancient and medieval culture has known this truth in some form; it is part of the primordial tradition, the perennial philosophy, the universal wisdom that underpins the old cultures with their

Introduction

different religions.... This revelation is...always available to each one of us, in every culture, in every time, in any moment of our lives. It is thus the first and permanent source of revelation."

We imagine ourselves to be modern humans, whatever that means — techno-marvels? brain masters? — but at the biological level, and in our quest for meaning, we are still Pleistocene people. Our minds trick us into believing we have achieved a certain heightened level of evolution, but our bodies tell us differently. That which moved us, informed us, inspirited us, and matured us hundreds of thousands of years ago remains unchanged: Nature remains the clean and pure page we write ourselves upon. She remains the bedrock of our human experience, the mother, father, and spirit revealed to us in physical forms we can touch and know in real-time communion.

She informs our dreams with her night sounds, infuses our days with everything we have come to know that endures — sunlight, breeze, soil, hard frost on autumn grasses. She births life in moisture and often straining, and takes it all back sometimes with fury. Somehow, in our ancient hearts and bones, we instinctively know that the glass-fragile days of our own lives mimic her in ways great and small, secular and spiritual, old and new.

Why Buffalo Dance

The deep and enduring questions — who we are, what we are, what is true, how we heal — are inseparable from our relationship with the natural world because we *are* the natural world. The percentage of our bodies that is salt water is the same as the proportion of the earth that is ocean. What is left of us is composed of minerals, in a proportion which mimics that of the surface of the earth. The water and clay that fashion us are given to us by the earth, and we, in turn, exchange our molecules with hers on a regular basis. We are, in effect, miniature living planets. The Original Instructions encoded within us for living in a good way are the same instructions that the planet follows: care for your children, take only what you need, keep your nest clean, support your community, be cautious but never fearful, trust life.

The Original Instructions — also called the Law of Life — are posted all around us in the form of living creatures, living systems, and living cycles. To tap into the wisdom of the Law, we need only remember where to look and how to ask.

The Lessons of the Seasons

This book presumes a distinctly cyclical — as opposed to linear — pattern to human life. The circle and spiral, which are cycles themselves, are some of the oldest universal symbols known to humankind and represent ultimate

cosmic order in nearly all early civilizations. In ancient Egypt, the number zero — the circle — was considered a holy place, the birthplace of all knowledge. The circle reveals unity, infinity, union, and motion (as the wheel). The circle is represented in human expression in countless forms, including labyrinths, wheels, mandalas, whirling dances, and medicine wheels. In nature, the circle reveals itself in such things as bird nests, wind patterns, tree trunks, fingerprints, planets, eyes, stones, and shells.

The geometric symbolism of the circle and square in conjunction — that is, a circle with four equidistant touch-points along its edge — is one of the oldest known symbols of the relationship between the finite and the infinite. It appears in the ancient art of Taoism, Islam, and Christianity and in the tribal traditions from which sprang all the world's religions. This ancient geometric symbol segments the circle neatly into four cardinal directions, or four seasons, illustrating the cycles of human life from birth to childhood, childhood to maturity, maturity to elderhood, and elderhood to death and rebirth. There are many symbols associated with the seasons. In nature, migration and hibernation are powerful symbols of autumn and winter. Flowers, hatching eggs, and ripe tomatoes carry the memories of spring and summer. In many traditions, the cardinal directions and their associated winds are the keepers of the seasons.

Why Buffalo Dance

Revealed in the cycle of the seasons is an enduring and profound wisdom for humankind as we spin our way through thousands of generations of births, deaths, and rebirths on the wheel of life. I can think of no other aspect of creation that speaks to us as urgently or compassionately about the necessity to live life with fullness and integrity as the song and pageantry of winter, spring, summer, and autumn.

With color, texture, temperature, motion, emotion, light, and sound, the seasons sing to us in a chorus of voices, harmonizing through a miraculous cast of characters who tread alongside us on the same journey from one sun to another. All living creatures follow their seasons of germination, growth, blossoming, ripening, and decay. It has always been this way and remains so: nature remains the first and best example of how to live, grow, prosper, accept, endure, and let go.

Each season is bequeathed an energy unique to it. Living in harmony with the energy patterns of each season, as all wild things do by nature, we can learn again how to synchronize our own lives with the larger life of the planet and to align ourselves with the distinct possibilities of each fourfold cycle.

Each season is given its own set of important tasks. If we — humans and squirrels alike — do not, for

instance, gather the harvests of fall, we will not survive the tasks of winter. If we — humans and robins alike — do not nurture our spring dreams, we will have nothing to hatch come the growing time of summer. Each season has its place in a larger sequence, as well. Winter cannot, according to the Law of Life, come after spring. The tasks of the seasons fall in a natural cycle, each building on the last and making ready for the next. In the seasons of our lives when we have witnessed uncommonly early springs, extraordinarily long winters, and shockingly unseasonal weather, we have seen, either in personal experience or in the news, the chaotic results — mudslides, floods, frozen crops, dangerous tides, drought.

Humans live two lives. One we share with the physical world. The other is lived inside us. In our inner worlds, we can rocket through all the energies of all the seasons in a day; sometimes in the midst of summer, we have our own private wintertime of deep silence. Still, what nature discloses to us from one season to the next holds true for our inner cycles, no matter how quickly — or slowly — we pass through them. The seasonal ripening, harvesting, and release must be mirrored in our inner journey *in task and in sequence*, because we are the earth in microcosm, physically and spiritually.

Story Keepers

Every species has its signature gift. The beaver is a master engineer, the falcon a master flyer, the lark a master singer. We humans are master storytellers and story keepers. Although many animals and even plants have elaborate communication practices, from sounds to dances to smells, no creature tells stories in the way that we do. Since humankind discovered language, we have been telling stories that inform, teach, inspire, chronicle, caution, heal, and — perhaps most important — create meaning out of a perpetual avalanche of events and information.

After experience, the next best thing is, I believe, a good story. In this volume, you have a collection of good stories given to me by badgers and bison, magpies and moose, eagles and elk. Over a period of fifteen years, while living in a series of mountain cabins on river edges, hilltops, and flats, I collected these stories from a host of wild beings who were gracious enough to spend some moments with me. Each creature ushered me into a deeper understanding of what life gives to us — and asks of us — as we participate in the universal dance of cycle and season. Sit quietly with the stories and listen until you can hear the grunting of the bear, the whistling of the hawk, and the chuckle of the coyote. When your ears become open to these voices, all your seasons will be the richer for it.

WINTER

WINTER

North Wind, all that you are —
Season of winter, house of white blizzards and stars, darkness
of deep night.
Dwelling place of the white buffalo and the snowy owl.
Guardian of the elders and the ancestors.
Place of essence, silence, purity, containment, courage, and
wisdom.
Home of death and rebirth.
The fallow time of the garden, skeletal trees, dormant seeds.
Whisper to us through this time of inner recollection and
silence.
Your energies are latent, potent, concentrated, and turned
within.
Grant that our harvest will sustain and preserve us through
short days
And long, long nights. Show us how to rest deeply and fully,
So that we may regenerate strong energy for the coming
sunrise fires of spring.
From the slumbering bear, may we come to more fully
understand
Sleep that looks like death, and rebirth that multiplies the self.
From the bare lands, may we be tutored by the mysterious
nurture of emptiness
And the close realms of spirit and mystery.
North Wind, blow through us. Bring us your blessings and
your wisdom.

ON MYSTERY
Winter Spirit

The country knows. If you do wrong things to it, the whole country knows. It feels what's happening to it. I guess that everything is connected together somehow, under the ground.

— LAVINE WILLIAMS, KOYUKON ELDER,
QUOTED BY RICHARD NELSON IN *ISLAND WITHIN*

THE SOUND OF LAUGHING bounced off rainbow-colored ice crystals in the midnight air. Janet had fallen into a pocket of deep, fluffy snow. Teresa was trying to pull her out, when she flopped over as well. Meanwhile, Arrow's broad, wiggling collie rump knocked me off balance and face-first into a drift.

We'd been told that on this night, after ten o'clock,

the full moon would be brighter and bigger than we would see it again in our lifetimes, so we decided to make a special night of it. Teresa wore a small blanket wrapped around her head. Janet was in fat-legged snow pants and a jacket three sizes too big for her. We wanted to be warm enough to sit still in temperatures way below freezing, so we all put on extra layers of whatever we could find, fashion police be damned. Dogs in tow, we headed up to the spring to sit on the old cistern and soak up moon magic.

Where the aspens met the pasture, an enormous chokecherry bush made an arch across the trail. All three of us stooped to pass under it. Janet called this "the portal." Ancient people believed that arches and over-hangs in nature represented entryways to sacred ground and alternate realms. I've taken to passing under portals of brush, stone, and water with a tingling, hushed sense of anticipation and excitement. My Celtic friend Frank would say, "You're crossing through the veil now."

Scooting under the sheltering arms of the choke-cherry, we settled into an unintentional silence. Only the snow made sounds as we walked, squeaking under our big boots. The dogs lined up behind us as we slipped into a small stand of aspens. Up in front, Teresa stopped suddenly to look straight up, and all of us — dogs, too — bunched up in a row behind her and stared upward as well. Arrow sniffed the air with her eyes full and expectant.

Tiny clumps of snow fell off the aspen limbs like slow-falling stars. Against the rising moon, tree branches stood out black and jointed, interlaced like ebony webbing. In the moonlight, the aspen trunks gleamed brighter even than the snow. Like tall porcelain figurines, the trees watched us. Some stood straight. Others bent at the hip, and some leaned forward as though they had something important to say.

Teresa set out again, and we continued our quiet way up the trail, eyes darting everywhere, shoulders scrunched up in wonder as if we were children in fairyland. The night air glowed blue-green and colored our lips purple and our skin the shade of mermaids underwater. Somewhere up the hill, an owl hooted, and two more answered from the east.

The moon spilled into the woods and across the pastures with light so bright that many of the stars slipped into hiding. Snow hushed the sound all around us, and what little sound we made seemed to remain flat up against our faces.

When I first followed the trail up to the spring and its cistern many seasons ago, I felt unsettled sitting up there. It was as though I were being constantly watched by something in the woods, and I had the eerie, prickling

sensation of eyes looking at me from every direction. The shamans say this means the place has a strong spirit, and the spirit is making itself known to you.

According to the theologian Thomas Moore, the Greeks took serious note of sensations universal in human experience and named them gods and goddesses, giving form to emotions. Sometimes it feels as though love has grasped us with a golden hand, or jealousy is literally wrapping itself around us. Thrift, vanity, power, innocence, beauty — how often have I felt myself in the literal grip of one of these, overtaken by an emotion that seems to have a life all its very own. Walking in the woods in the dark can easily turn emotions into presences, and when Strongheart nuzzled me from behind, he just as easily could have been the god of the aspens as my dog. At 160 pounds and pure white, Strongheart, an Anatolian shepherd, had more than a bit of Zeus in him.

We reached the cistern just after midnight. The shadows of everything commingled into startling shapes that might have lumbered off into a creature life of their very own. None of us had said a word since our laughing fit at the bottom of the hill. Now we began to speak of the presence of this moonlit place, as though the spears of moonbeams had prodded it, and everything in it, to life.

We leaned over the edge of the cistern, taking off

our heavy gloves and cupping handfuls of ice-cold water that gushed from the runoff spout. The water on my hands had a quality unique to itself, as did the fresh snow cushioning my seat. The trees and the boulders, the night air, the shafts of moonlight — each I could imagine in its own god or goddess dress, animated and alive.

I shared my thoughts with Teresa and Janet. Teresa suggested that not only was each of these things a spirit in itself but also the place — all of it — was a spirit, too. Her observation reminded me instantly that each place I've loved seemed like a treasured relative, with its own character, mood, and quirks.

Winter, too, is her own self, dressed in muted, two-dimensional tones, silent, thoughtful, receptive but not engaging. She is all these things and more, but at her core — which I could see clearly in the nondark — she is deeply mysterious, as shadows are mysterious and austerity is mysterious. Little shields us from the inscrutability of winter, and we enter her world with a sense of marvel, resignation, and awe. It is the cold time, the time of preservation and conservation, when the sap drains from the trees and the animals rest, sleep, and endure. But it is also the most mysterious of the seasons, a time when the veil between this world and the world of spirit is as thin as hoarfrost.

7

Why Buffalo Dance

As the biggest, closest moon of our lives shone down on us, we three women sat soaking up the rare moments. Night, moonlight, and snow combined in an intimate embrace, birthing spirits all over the land. I looked at Strongheart and thought how perfect it would be if he were to start one of his long, melodic howls, but he didn't, so we women howled instead, over and over, singing a spirit song of winter.

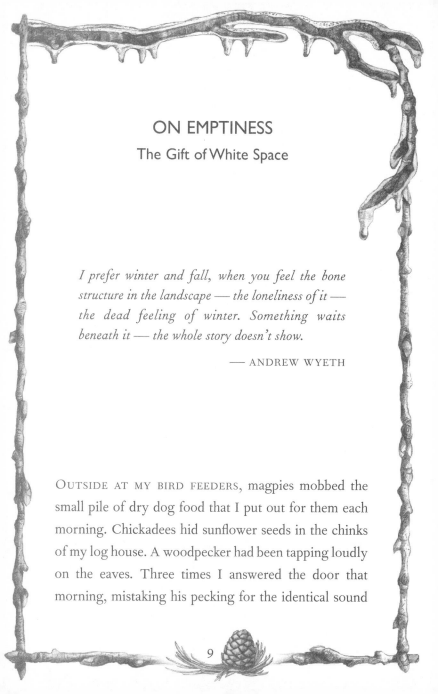

ON EMPTINESS
The Gift of White Space

I prefer winter and fall, when you feel the bone structure in the landscape — the loneliness of it — the dead feeling of winter. Something waits beneath it — the whole story doesn't show.

— ANDREW WYETH

OUTSIDE AT MY BIRD FEEDERS, magpies mobbed the small pile of dry dog food that I put out for them each morning. Chickadees hid sunflower seeds in the chinks of my log house. A woodpecker had been tapping loudly on the eaves. Three times I answered the door that morning, mistaking his pecking for the identical sound of the woodpecker door knocker on the front door. Maybe a doorbell would be a better idea.

The elk, deer, and moose had traveled down from the high country. The colder the days, the less they moved about. Earlier in the week, I had seen a bull moose out browsing on bitterbrush. His antlers were enormous, and his body bigger than my car. As the weather grew harsher, he'd move off the sage flats and into the willow bushes.

Snow rose up like a tide against the foundation of the cabin and drifted up in waves around the porch stairs like sea foam caressing a lighthouse. On stormless days, Arrow and Strongheart walked with me along the edges of alfalfa and hay pastures to look over oceans of white. Except for the crisscross of animal tracks, the surface of the snowfields was unbroken. Four ponds of various sizes surrounded by cattails marked the corners of the pastureland. I especially liked to visit the one with the old Windsurfer board frozen into its surface.

In summer, these same pastures teem with hawks, coyotes, birdsong, grasses, and insect calls, but in winter it's an entirely different, sparsely populated landscape. Winter is the time of year when the word *empty* comes to mind. The crayon box of the seasons has been stripped of all but a few colors. Someone — autumn, I think — grabbed all the oranges, the yellows, and the burnt siennas and left nothing but sepia, white, gray, and a very somber dark green. The busy textures and sounds of the other seasons have been obliterated by a determined flood of snow. *Empty*. This is what the pastures said to me.

I used to fear that word, even the very thought of it. I would fill up emptiness wherever I found it — with conversation, ideas, plans, furniture, lists of things to do, a vase full of fresh sage and juniper twigs. If I couldn't fill emptiness with things, I would fill it up with feelings of anxiety, because, given its cultural connotation, *empty* stands right beside such words as *lacking, barren, meaningless*. When we make New Year's resolutions, we don't normally say, "I resolve to make my life empty this year." When we pray, we don't pray to be unfilled or vacant.

But this has become my personal wish this winter: to keep some empty space inside myself. Here in high country that seems to glory in its near-endless winters, the passage of the long white months forces me to sit with a new, more expansive vision of emptiness. New possibilities begin to emerge around an old and feared concept. In the bitter cold days, when so many animals have up and left the area, and the season presses her white-gloved hands over every hint of life. I see that in the stripping away of the ornamentation of leaves,

flowers, and summer sounds, winter has created a landscape of essence. The very whiteness and openness of it all is a visual celebration of purity and self-recollection. The distractions are all gone. The canvas has been prepared for the next painting.

Essence is the place that lies beneath the bedrock of everything that is. With a frosty whisper, the pastures remind me that emptiness is about hands opened and upturned in acceptance and wonder to claim the unadorned truth and essential nature of life.

Winter comes wrapped not in a fancy package but in a dress of elegant simplicity. I am trying to cultivate more of this rich landscape of emptiness *as essence* in my life — both in my actions and in my thinking. It is not easy, because winter is not easy. In graphic design classes, I was told that the most important elements on the page are not the words or the photos but the white space — the space you left empty.

Winter — the giant of white space.

Like the moose at this time of year, I celebrate being still. Like the chickadees, I fill my days with fewer activities. Eating, sleeping, enjoying hot showers and the glow of yellow fires are all richer moments when surrounded by more white space. I pare away errands and movie nights. I create broad swaths of snowfields between my activities, because my soul needs such things. She needs this wintertime to digest all of summer's past dreams and surprises. I am, like a hibernating ground squirrel, full up with a year's busyness and feasting, and I need this blessed time of emptying, of stillness, and of space.

A grouse dives head-first into the snow, plowing a burrow beneath the surface to insulate herself from the cold world above. She sits there quietly for hours or days, surrounded by no color, no song, no motion, and fills herself up with silence. She has secrets to share, and one of them is about the deep rest of white space.

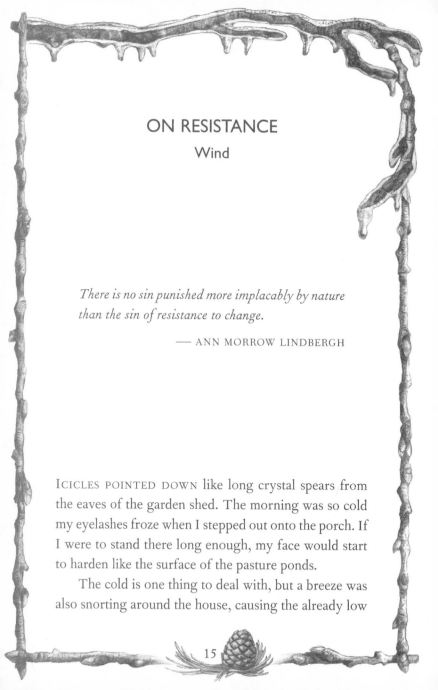

ON RESISTANCE
Wind

There is no sin punished more implacably by nature than the sin of resistance to change.

— ANN MORROW LINDBERGH

ICICLES POINTED DOWN like long crystal spears from the eaves of the garden shed. The morning was so cold my eyelashes froze when I stepped out onto the porch. If I were to stand there long enough, my face would start to harden like the surface of the pasture ponds.

The cold is one thing to deal with, but a breeze was also snorting around the house, causing the already low temperatures to plummet. When wind starts early in the morning, it can be churning up snowdrifts by afternoon. At the very thought of a stinging blow, I braced myself. I used to have horses and donkeys, and I would hunch myself against the weather twice a day to feed them. Wind would pile snowdrifts up in minutes, making the journey of a few hundred yards to the barn seem like a trek to the base of Everest.

I no longer have anything to feed outside but birds during the winter, yet I don't resist the wind any less. Standing on the porch while scooping out a bucket of sunflower seeds, I felt my body preparing itself automatically for the cold gusts. My face scrunched up, my neck retracted inside my jacket. I hunched my shoulders, put my head down, and charged stoically into the press of the blow, heading for the swinging feeders a few yards away. The wind hit me with a *whoosh*, and the sound of it bunched up my already tense muscles all the tighter. Everything in my body resisted, from my face, to my ears, to my clenched hands. Like a reluctant boxer, I felt as if I'd been sent out to battle an adversary who always wins.

The tubular feeders swayed in the wind, and I grabbed them and pulled them off the tree limbs and feeder poles. Placing them between my knees one at a time, I removed the tops and poured in the sunflower seed with a small scoop. Much of it fell to the ground, where the finches would pounce on it as soon as I left. I held my breath against the wind that pushed me from the side like playful hands. Up in the dead aspen that serves as a large perch, the birds watched me curiously, their heads darting from side to side, some of them extending their necks to get a better look at breakfast.

I watched them back, thinking they didn't look very tense at all. While my eyes squinted, theirs were round and bright. I stood all pretzel-shaped and tense, and they sat fluffy and soft-looking around the edges. Behind them, toward the back of the yard, another visitor suddenly caught my eye. Blinking against the gale, I was surprised to see a cow moose nestled drowsily in the snow by the willows. She's been a visitor for years, but each time I see her, I am startled all over again by her size and her simple presence in this neighborhood of cabins and dogs. Half-covered with a dusting of blown snow, she moved her chin from side to side while she chewed a mouthful of regurgitated willow twigs. If I could have named her expression, I would have called it bliss. I couldn't help but compare her attitude with mine.

Around me, a family of magpies danced on the wind, their impossibly long tails sailing out behind them like black ribbons. While the wind dropped them, hurtled them, rocketed them up, the birds held out their wings and made tiny adjustments with their necks, feet, and elbows.

Something in the moment beckoned me to try this myself. I put down the bucket and tried to stand with my arms out, my face soft, and my attitude open instead of braced. I relaxed my eye muscles. Instantly, my whole mood shifted as my body tried on the new posture. It was not so difficult to let the wind just have me. I smiled and let my shoulders drop. Cold air blasted around my chin, and I let loose and swallowed it. A shiver grabbed me, and I tensed for a moment, then relaxed again, surprised to find it possible to shiver with loose limbs.

I looked over my shoulder and watched as the moose kept chewing and flipped her funnel ears toward and away from the blowing weather. I have seen animals still as stones in winter, but never can I recall them in a posture of utter resistance. On the elk refuge, the elk stand and kneel facing the wind, their eyes soft and reflective. In the frigid waters of the rivers, I sometimes see the shadowy bodies of trout stretched out, sleek and supple. The shivering birds quake like lithe dancers, dip their heads round and tuck them deep into their feathers with the serenity of a yoga master.

I experimented with my body and braced myself again, tensing, hardening, curling up like a sow bug. On the heels of my posture change, anxiety and something akin to anger blew into every crack of my exposed skin. I gave the wind a name, and it was not a kind one. Releasing a deep breath, I sighed and leaned into the arms of the gale as though she were a kindly friend, and felt my name for her change into something more respectful.

Resistance takes energy, and winter is hardly a time to waste energy on something as useless as denial. The Buddha says that all suffering comes from wanting things to be different than they are. The wind and the cold are real. So are hunger and loss. What is the value in using precious energy to resist what is true?

The magpies were getting annoyed, eager for me to leave so they could eat. I picked up my empty bucket and turned back to the house, walking with my body slack and my neck soft, and for just that moment the wind didn't feel nearly so cold.

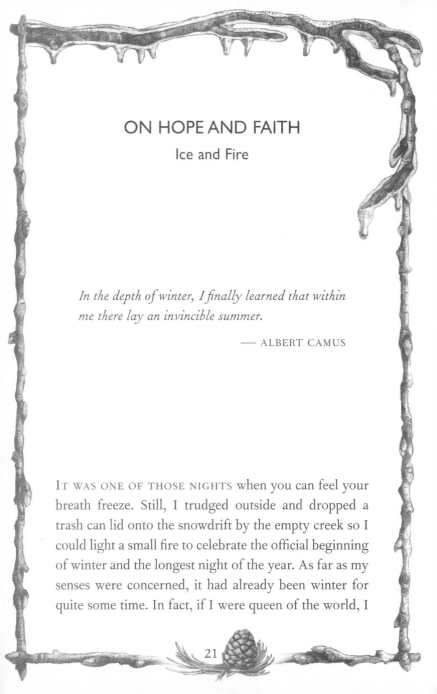

ON HOPE AND FAITH
Ice and Fire

In the depth of winter, I finally learned that within me there lay an invincible summer.

— ALBERT CAMUS

IT WAS ONE OF THOSE NIGHTS when you can feel your breath freeze. Still, I trudged outside and dropped a trash can lid onto the snowdrift by the empty creek so I could light a small fire to celebrate the official beginning of winter and the longest night of the year. As far as my senses were concerned, it had already been winter for quite some time. In fact, if I were queen of the world, I would decree that winter would begin sometime in November, when everything that says *winter* to me is already firmly in place.

Ice crystals and tiny icicles danced on the bare limbs of willow bushes and fell with a tinkle when I bumped against them. The air — brittle and sharp — might have broken had I moved through it too quickly. The surface of the snow was unmarred by a single track, and the night was soundless except for the popping of the fire I built quickly with wood I keep stored in the shed for just such an occasion.

According to a native folktale I once read, stars can come to earth and become round, furry, puppylike creatures with turtle heads. The puppy-stars shoot off sparks as they roll about. They can return to the heavens whenever they choose. Children love them. But no stars came down to visit me. Instead, I had the company of my two dogs, Strongheart and Arrow, and they rolled about in the snow but stayed far enough from the fire — thankfully — that they didn't spark. I always worry about Arrow's tail. It is a thick fur plume, and she waves it everywhere. It's gotten singed more than once.

Skies are brilliant up in the mountains, and on clear, cold nights they take your breath away. Strongheart plowed over to me and shoved his cold nose against my cheek. It stung like an ice cube. How do dogs keep their noses from freezing? Already, my own was getting tingly and numb.

All around me in the bare limbs of cottonwoods and aspens, in cracks of trunks and house eaves, in the thick of the spruces, packed together in birdhouses, birds were sleeping. I couldn't see a one of them, but I knew they were there, preserving their energy until morning light. If they ran out of fuel — stored food energy — before morning, ice might find them and touch their small hearts with her cold fingers, and they would not see another sunrise. I have found birds some mornings, frozen solid like colored stones. For a tiny bird huddled in the dark, each night must seem like a full winter, each sunrise a spring.

Birds have the gift of insulating feathers. Many have the ability to drop their body temperatures at night. Their legs and feet are small, scaly tubes of fat and bone, for the most part highly resistant to frostbite. Insulating fat circles their hearts, and a high daytime metabolism energizes them in their ceaseless quest for food. All these things and many more help them keep the insistent hands of ice at bay.

I poked at my sparse fire, which wasn't casting enough heat to keep my feet warm, and wondered aloud to the dogs what gifts the cosmos had given me to survive the grip of deep ice — not the kind of ice that I thwart with fleece and wool but the presences that feel like ice, and that can freeze a human heart when the dark nights of the soul are very long.

I stabbed the fire again, harder, and sparks danced like ghosts above the flames. Melancholy, shame, helplessness, profound injustice: these are a few of the cold spirits that can poke a sharp, thin icicle into the heart and freeze the very life out of it.

I watched the sparks die, become bits of icy ash, and settle in shadowy blots on the snow. *Hello, depression! Remember when you came and stayed and stayed? Shame. Go away. I never want to speak to you. You always show up at the worst times.* There must be gifts, I thought, ripened in me over the centuries to protect my core from these dead-cold visitors that can make any season feel like winter. What insulates my heart?

An answer came to me unexpectedly. I cocked my head to hear an owl in the far distance. On clear nights, sound travels a long way. I uncovered my ears and listened more closely: *Whoot-whoo-whoo-whoot-whoot.* Shortly, they'd be calling to each other, signifying the beginning of another breeding season. As the longest night stretched out in front of me, the owl's call hinted of a time to come when the ice would be gone, eggs would hatch, and owlets would trill. Great horned owls are harbingers of transition, the first creatures here to give voice to the growing season just around the bend. They are also associated with the transformation of life into death, and so touch each season of life with their haunting calls.

Many times I could not imagine anything existing beyond the dark, threatening seasons of my life. Those days were like living in a perpetual ice age, when my interior heat was constantly in danger of being snuffed out by the spirit of deep inner cold. On every horizon, icicles seemed to surround me, dangling from sky to earth, and the warmth of hope was a dim faltering light.

Hopelessness is like getting your skin wet and exposed in winter — all the heat leaches out of you, and the ice finds your heart, and that is that. But on solstice night, I heard the faint hooting of the owl. Even more than that, I heard the promise of renewal whispered in the tones of his call. Perhaps I heard him because I had lived through a half century of winters, and my ears were open to a simple faith that winter ends and hope lives.

Hope is not a gift we can sustain simply by our own will. Hope is something we need to hear from outside ourselves sometimes. Like the fire needs the help of a branch to grow its warmth, we need a voice sometimes, or a sight, or visitor, to fan the flicker in our hearts when faith grows dim. On solstice, the voice came to me in the call of the owl, but nature has endless other voices that speak of hope: the sound of water to a thirsty creature, the breath of sunshine on a cold one, the call of kin and kind to one who is lost.

The owl's hoot — more a vibration than a sound — wrapped around me like a down cape, insulating me from the most chilling of life's spirits. *This melancholy will end. The darkness of loss will find its way to light again. This wound will be healed someday. The cold will move on.*

I wondered if the winter creatures felt the thrumming hoot of the owl in their own hearts. Perhaps the call settled into their bodies as a small fire, much like the gift of hope that warms me through the most frigid of inner nights. Yet if the owl call touched them, it touched them as a remembrance of what they already knew on faith alone. So untarnished is their covenant with life, they endure on unwavering faith, not as a mental construct, but as a felt knowing. For me, for all humankind, there remains the gift of hope when faith wears thin. I don't know how long I sat listening to the owls, watching my small fire glow, then fade. I didn't look at a clock before I went outside, and I would not look at one when I got back into the house. When the last ember died, I woke the dogs and headed back to the cabin, carrying the owl's small fire in my cold hands.

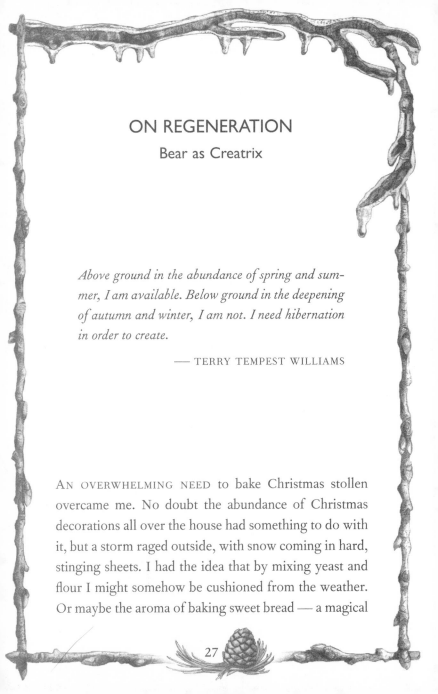

ON REGENERATION
Bear as Creatrix

*Above ground in the abundance of spring and sum-
mer, I am available. Below ground in the deepening
of autumn and winter, I am not. I need hibernation
in order to create.*

— TERRY TEMPEST WILLIAMS

AN OVERWHELMING NEED to bake Christmas stollen
overcame me. No doubt the abundance of Christmas
decorations all over the house had something to do with
it, but a storm raged outside, with snow coming in hard,
stinging sheets. I had the idea that by mixing yeast and
flour I might somehow be cushioned from the weather.
Or maybe the aroma of baking sweet bread — a magical

potion if ever there was one — would ensure my insulation from the gale outside.

Strongheart waved his tail by the door and looked at me with a lopsided grin. When I opened it for him, he gazed out for a second or two, backed up, and slunk apologetically toward the heating stove. A big, active lunk of a dog, he preferred to sleep away stormy days. In an instant, he was stretched out by the heater, his breath slowing down to a rumbling snore like a train pulling into the station. I knew exactly how he felt. Everything outside reflected the idea of rest, conservation, storing of energy. Winter is the only season when I don't feel guilty about sleeping late, yawning a lot, and working less.

From the pantry, I pulled out the big bucket of bread flour. Arrow came to watch for a moment, hoping a dog biscuit might be on the menu. I handed her a Christmas cookie instead, and she pranced all around the kitchen, her collie tail waving like a victory flag, before swallowing it whole. Arrow had the good sense — and the bladder control — not to even suggest to me that she would like to go out.

I glanced over to where Strongheart lay like a huge, torpid bear, doing his own version of hibernation. His feet twitched in a dream. While I watched, his eyelids fluttered and his nose crinkled up. If his ears and tail had been shorter, he'd look just like a polar bear. I almost named him that — Bear — not just because of his size but also because, in traditions the world over, the bear is the symbol of many powerful things, and Strongheart certainly was a powerful dog.

One of the most compelling myths is Bear as dreamer of life. Certain native people of this country observe that Sow Bear goes into a sleep as deep as death and brings forth life — cubs — in the process. The first people must have marveled at the bear's long gestation cycle. Bears mate in spring yet do not appear with young until the following spring. Nature has given sow bears the ability to delay implantation of their fertilized eggs until after they have entered their dens for the winter. Only then do the eggs find a home on the walls of their mothers' uteruses. In myth, the grizzly goes into her long winter sleep and dreams her babies into existence.

I worked my dough on a marble slab given to me by a good friend exactly for this purpose. The stone has a spider webbing of gray and white, just like the day's skies. The dough was vanilla colored and smelled like flowers and beer. I greased a midnight blue ceramic bowl with butter and plopped the dough ball in the middle, turning it over so that some of the butter covered the top to keep it from drying out. Then I covered the bowl and set it next to the crèche, which stood by the heating stove. Mirella was curled up in her dress of gray tiger stripes in the middle of the manger scene, purring. Somehow, she had managed to avoid knocking over Jesus and the angels, but a plaster donkey and sheep had fallen to the floor.

Out in the woods, perhaps at the very moment my stollen was dreaming its yeasty dreams, miracles were happening in bear land. Deep in their winter caves, their bodies a few degrees below normal, their breathing slow, the grizzly bears slept. Above them, winter storms moved through the land, trailing banshee veils of white. Except for the raven's harsh call, the forest sat silent. On ponds where thermal springs kept away the snow, trumpeter swans bent down their glistening white necks and pulled up plants as mists rose up around them like breath.

Within the bear caves, the cosmic pageant of death, birth, and rebirth was playing out. Tiny grizzly cubs, naked, blind, and the size of a large fist, slid their hot, viscous way into the world. Their mothers slept on, unknowing and unmoving, their bodies and dreams still caught fast in the grip of hibernation.

The diminutive cubs, from one to four in number, would crawl from their dark, moist places of entry, grope their way up the bellies of their slumbering mothers until they found a nipple, and grab on. By the time the sow bears awakened a few months later, the cubs would be furry balls of squiggling life, ready to make their first forays out into the remnants of a winter wonder world.

In the bowl by the heater, the dough quickly began to rise like a pregnant belly, and I wondered if dreams were gestating and swelling inside me while I danced my own peculiar hibernation waltz. A part of me sleeps through the winter, the part that craves mental activity, new projects, and the incessant action of summer. I putter with smaller projects: crafts, writing, reading — activities close to my den. I even listen to different music, attracted especially to chants even during the Christmas season: Gregorian, Hindu, African, Buddhist, and the Taize chants I sang on a ten-day silent retreat months before.

While I separated and shaped the spongy dough into four half-circle loaves, I remembered those days in retreat and was suddenly aware that this day, with the stollen and the sleeping dogs and ideas of hibernation and birthing bears, had very much the same quality as those days of silence, prayer, and reflection.

Winter carries the evolutional, seasonal energy for deep rest and retreat from the world. Bears and many other animals in the North honor this period of rest and renewal in the act of hibernation. Throughout history,

across time and culture, humans have enacted hibernation through retreat. Like hibernation, retreat asks us to pare away the outside trappings and sustain and restore ourselves with what we have contained and stored inside. Like hibernation, retreat is a mysterious and pregnant process.

I painted the elliptical loaves with egg white while my mind wove its own myth about how humankind came to know retreat, darkness, renewal. Perhaps seeing Bear crawl into her months of solitary seclusion gave some fervent seeker the model for monasticism. Bear's wintering place — a cave or den — became the chosen destination of thousands of seekers across time for retreat and contemplation.

After the stollen went into the oven, I climbed the stairs to my room and grabbed a small statue of a sleeping bear. Returning downstairs, I knelt in front of the crèche, lifted Mirella out gently, and placed her on the recliner. Scooting aside the straw near Mary, I set down the statue of the bear. Two mothers were in the stable now, two dreams of a dark winter and a glorious spring, two sacred stories of birth, death, and rebirth.

ON REPRIEVE

The Chase

Life is not a spectacle or a feast; it is a predicament.

— GEORGE SANTAYANA

JUST BEYOND THE PASTURE, at the edge where the aspens and pines lined up like a row of conservatively garbed chorus girls, the ground rose up gently like the soft folds of a flannel skirt. The hushed trees extended welcoming arms there, and sunlight drifted through the branches and settled on the snow with ripple patterns.

It was late afternoon, and I'd set aside writing for

the day to walk the dogs up the hill and into the trees, all the way to the small spring that bubbles up from the soil and runs into the concrete cistern. The spring is the water source for a group of houses just down the road. It is the only natural source of water I drink from outdoors these days. The risk of bacteria in wild waters is too high.

I made my way to the spring by means of a narrow, winding path that my feet and the dogs' had packed by constant use. I didn't need snowshoes to come to this place, not even after a good snow dump. In winter, snow nearly fills the little gully where the spring erupts in a soft gurgle of bubbles. Peering over the edge of the snowbank, I smiled at the silver thread of moving water that wound into the cistern, gushed through the spill pipe at the other end, and coursed down the hill-side, where it eventually petered out at the edge of the pasture.

I loved the sound of the spring, like soft wind chimes made of glass. Chokecherry and serviceberry bushes that clustered along the spring's edge still carried some shriveled fruit, stuck like black peppercorns to the naked twigs. A raven called overhead, and his raspy voice echoed off the rocky sides of the ravine.

Strongheart sprinted ahead up the hill on legs like hinged stilts. Arrow was content to roll around in the snow, sliding along on her sides and back like a snow-drunk otter. I dusted the snow off a small corner of the cistern and sat, legs crossed, marveling at the wonder-land of white tree trunks, evergreen boughs swaying gently like deep-green ostrich feather fans, and silver water that rose up pure and clear from the mouth of the planet.

My reverie was cut short by a clatter of noise off to my right. In his meanderings, Strongheart had inadver-tently flushed a good-size buck mule deer. Exploding from a small stand of aspens up the hill, the buck sprang my way. Strongheart's head whipped up and he dove after the deer in slow-motion bounds. I could tell by his wide, goofy grin that he thought this was a game, but I knew it was no game for the deer.

I opened my mouth to holler, "No!" but before I could get out a sound, the buck twisted round to face my dog. Strongheart careened to a stop not fifteen feet away. The deer danced forward on stiff legs, stamping his hard feet in warning. Confused, but still stepping for-ward with that "Aw, shucks" wiggle in his shoulders, Strongheart hung out his pink tongue like a truce flag. The buck answered by dropping his head and waving his antlers, like a finger waggling side to side, saying, "Uh-uh." Shooting an apologetic glance my way, as though he'd gotten himself into an embarrassing situation,

Strongheart sat down in the snow in front of the buck. I could hear him whine softly.

The buck held his magnificent body tall and tight. He took two quick steps forward, leading with his branch of sharp, threatening spears. Strongheart scooted his behind backward in the snow like a clumsy plow. He whined again, softly, an imploring look in his black eyes. The buck jerked his head back up, as though he'd been hit on the forehead with a tiny pebble. Suddenly, against all logic, he relaxed, and his rigid muscles melted like butter before my eyes. Strongheart sniffed deeply, sucking in the rich, woodsy smells of the buck, and gently thrust his muzzle in the deer's direction. Hauling his large white rump off the ground, my dog turned away from the deer and trotted back toward me. The buck turned away, too, and stepped softly off toward the trees on the other side of the ravine, walking as though he hadn't a care in the world, as though a woman and two dogs were not watching mere yards away. I sat back straight and wide-eyed. The moment made no sense to me, and yet something about it sent shivers of recognition down my back like the tremors of a tuning fork.

I hadn't taken a breath during the entire interchange, and the air spilled out of my lungs with a *whoosh*. I thought, *Cancer was like that*. Not so many years back, I was a deer-person pursued by a hulking, ghost-colored thing at my back. Surely, I would be killed. It is what I was told again and again. In winter, doesn't the predator always overtake the snowbound, flailing prey?

It all seemed to happen so fast, then. Surgeries, treatments, searching, fear, all these things like wet snow grabbing at my ankles and pulling me under while the predator raced unimpeded on broad, hairy feet across the surface of the snow toward me.

Eventually, there is nothing to do, of course, but to turn and face what is after you, so there was a time for me of turning, of stopping like the deer.

Perhaps there is no other season in which fortune and providence are so keenly etched and the windfall of grace so acutely felt. Against a backdrop of biting white, everything suddenly stands out and nothing is obscured. Every bit of grace is sensed and cherished in a way unlike at any other time of life. The deer could not know, I told myself, that my dog was not death. And yet there was a mysterious moment when they both knew exactly that. In the bright and lucid transparency of winter, the buck heard that whisper from predator to prey. *Not now. Not you. Only turn around and look at me.* And the buck did, and there was peace and quiet, blessing and reprieve.

Reprieve. I found it too, that winter of my illness. There was a moment in which I knew it, just as surely as the buck knew it. Not because of worthiness, or accident, or swiftness was I pardoned, but by a simple, astounding gift of grace. That near-soundless whisper said to me, *Not now. Only turn and look at me.*

That voice speaks in all seasons, in different words, offering perhaps more subtle gifts of mercy. But in the warm months, it is easy to hear instead the sound of thundering water and the cacophony of birdcall. It is in the starkness of winter that we are able to recognize the sweet sigh of grace when she finds us, a sudden burst of miraculous, unexpected security in a landscape of cold and danger.

Strongheart trotted over to me, very pleased with himself. The chase after the buck left him panting and smiling, and he batted at me in play with a paw the size of my hand. Arrow was trembling head to foot, having restrained herself from joining in the mad dash after the deer. Her excited eyes now followed the buck into the woods and she whined softly, but I headed onto the path to home and called both dogs to follow.

Reprieve is an enigmatic thing, a sacred, inexplicable thing, and when it comes in winter moments of our lives, the bold taste of it on the tongue is unmistakable and precious.

ON RIGHT TIMING
Rock Courtship of Eagles

Just as no amount of effort will block the tide, no amount of effort will bring an event to fruition before its time.

— DANIEL QUINN, *THE TALES OF ADAM*

I COULD NOT STOP MYSELF from looking at the buds on the aspens several times a day to see if they'd fattened any. They are great teaser trees, setting out small versions of their buds before winter to torment me for six months with dreams of springtime. I'm a West Coast girl, raised where daffodils poke up out of the ground in

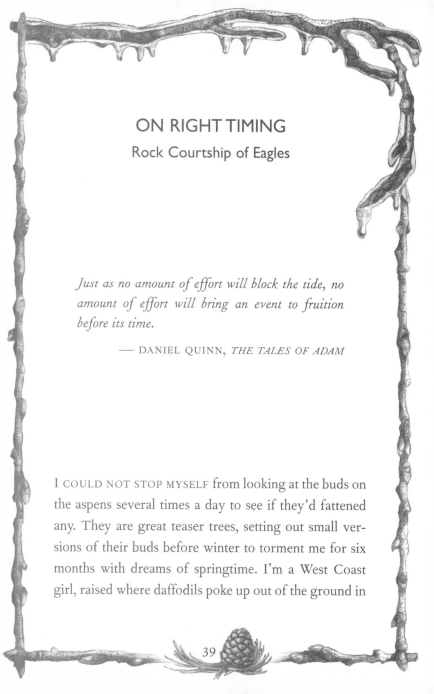

February, and crocuses even before that. While my body assured me that spring was in the air, most of the evidence outside kept telling me that it was not.

On a morning of blowing snow, and icicles dangling from the bird feeders, my heart and my eyes were in battle, and my eyes were winning. I could not deny the winter still in evidence all around me, yet yesterday on the elk refuge, I watched in amazement as two golden eagles mated. With my binoculars, I saw them sitting on the outermost craggy edge of a butte, indistinguishable from the rocks all around them except for their subtle movements. They sat side by side for the longest time, moving closer together in incremental steps the distance of a finger's width.

When their shoulders touched, the male — usually just a breath smaller than the female — reached out and gently began preening the short, arrow-shaped feathers of her head. In turn, she bent her neck to allow him better access. As she lowered her head, I saw her cere flash brilliant yellow like a small shaft of gold in stone.

The male shifted slightly, and with no fanfare he eased up onto the female's slender shoulders. His claws touched her back, dark wings cloaklike and spreading awkwardly for balance. I saw the female raise her tail swiftly as the male swayed back and forth once, then twice, and then it was over. In the span of only a moment, the male was settling down next to the female again, both of them ruffling their feathers back into shape.

I could scarcely believe what I'd seen, in part because the tryst was so fleeting. But also because it was so unexpected, a quick blast of heat in stark contrast with the ashen, cold surroundings. On my porch that morning, the memory seemed all the more surreal.

On the refuge, elk still roamed, a lazy wave. Their coats were thick and bristly like shaving brushes, and they sported winter colors of soft tan and creamy white. I was missing the sight of them in full sable summer pelage, missing the smell of grass that always surrounded them then, and missing the shiny, almost reflective sleekness they shared with all the summer mammals, from foxes to marmots.

In the field next door, three horses had their noses in a pile of hay, their rumps turned toward me, fuzzy as rabbits. A flicker made his way up the fence post, hanging on like an elegant tick, progressing upward by a series of tiny leaps and grabs. When he went back down the post, he simply fell by tiny increments, his black feet reaching out again and again like small grappling hooks.

Flickers are beautiful when they flash their wings, all fire-red underneath, but my heart was longing for the molten yellow and black of the meadowlark, the green uprising of skunk cabbage spears, and the smell of dirt.

Why Buffalo Dance

It's not time, the snow seemed to say. Not time? The idea agitated me as much as the cold did. Why not? It was time for the eagles yesterday!

I saw them instantly in my memory, joined, teetering, all wing and muscle. The words of Rolling Thunder, a Cherokee holy man, came to me. He had spoken once about the idea of timing, and about how the right timing of all things was so very important. All the good deeds in the world, he claimed, were useless if their timing was not right. And the right thing at the wrong time was not the right thing at all.

I flung handfuls of sunflower seeds onto the falling snow, and instantly a riot of rosy finches appeared, massing on the ground like a scattering of jumbled thoughts. *It was time for the eagles yesterday*. Yes, it was time. Eagle hearts are exquisitely tuned to nature's gentle urgings. It was time. Just as surely as it was not yet time for the lark, the skunk cabbage, or the dirt. For an instant I imagined their returning at the wrong time. The lark freezes at midnight and falls off the fence railing, a tumbling yellow planet striking the snow. The shoots of skunk cabbage wither like crumpled, brown paper. The dirt turns lifeless and hard.

In my mind's ear, I heard my boyfriend tell me, "It's just not time yet," when I confided to him that I didn't know which way my life was calling me to turn, and that

I wondered why nothing was showing itself as a comforting signpost. A good friend asked me why she remained partnerless after years of fruitless searching, and I heard myself say to her, "It's not time yet."

Above the beams on the porch sat old robins' nests. I had left them there to remind me of spring and the urgent squeaks of baby birds. They remained empty because it was not time yet. I wondered if the elk or the foxes felt the same urgency I did to merge my impatient heart and my undeniable vision into a united whole. But I suspected they were the ones who taught Rolling Thunder about the importance of right timing in the first place.

Spring is loaded with surprises, possibilities, great expectations and ideas, unexpected dreams, and bushels of life, but this treasure chest opens not according to our timetable, which is often just the child of our impatience, but to the mysterious call of right timing. Utterly out of our control, right timing must be acknowledged, respected, and accepted. It will not be harnessed, and it is usually recognized and understood only after it has arrived or passed.

Arrow pushed the door open and rushed out to greet me, the entire back half of her body wagging as strongly as the tail behind it. Was it time for a walk? This is what she asks of me most mornings. "Yes, Arrow," I said to her, "it's exactly the right time."

SPRING

SPRING

East Wind, all that you are —
Season of springtime, house of yellow warmth, dawning
of day, home of the sunrise fires.
Dwelling place of the eagle and the hawk.
Guardian of the infants.
Place of new beginnings, fresh dreams, and rising sap,
The planting of seeds, and the birth of young.
Guide us through this time of rekindled hope and
freshening light.
Help us to find the dreams and tasks that are ours for
the coming year
And to balance ourselves carefully between focus and
flexibility.
Show us how to move your unbridled creative energy
through our hearts and bodies
As surely as the deer move through labor and birth,
As phlox opens to its flowering.
Keep us steeped in our wildness for at least this one
season
So that our dreams are not domesticated or
restrained.
East Wind, blow through us. Bring us your blessings and
your wisdom.

ON PLAY AND FROLIC
Buffalo Gals, Won't You Come Out Tonight

...and dance by the light of the moon.

BISON DON'T FROLIC. That was the thought running through my head while, before my eyes, a bison performed a tap dance on a picnic table. I was having a hard time reconciling what I was seeing with what I believed. Meanwhile, the buffalo leaped about on the table, bobbing his huge head back and forth, occasionally leaping into the air like a way-oversized Baryshnikov.

Why Buffalo Dance

I had taken a day off to drive north. Although spring had begun to extend herself into my valley, up in the national park winter hung on a bit longer. Snowdrifts, hardened like piles of white plaster, nearly obscured the tables in the picnic area where I stopped to stretch my legs. A heavy crunching sound off to my left signaled the arrival of a small herd of bedraggled bison. Through a curtain of lodgepole pines, they emerged and aimed their shaggy heads my way.

Instantly, I moved, giving them plenty of room. Buffalo are about the size of small cars, but there is nothing machinelike in their attitude. I control the keys to my car, but no one controls the keys to the buffalo. Too big a handful for most predators, too strong for most fences, too wild to be confused with cattle, buffalo pretty much do what they want. What they wanted that sunny afternoon, it seemed, was to picnic.

From the shelter of the trees, I watched them while they congregated around the barbecue pits and snow-piled wooden tables. One stopped to scratch her absurdly small behind against a bench, and I could hear the scritch-scritching noises of fur against wood. They are unlikely looking animals. I've always thought they looked a bit like front-end loaders, like they might tip over onto their noses, but somehow they manage to balance that enormous refrigerator of a head over feet the size of tuna cans.

The back end of the bison is clearly an afterthought. All creation's time and energy was spent on the curving horns, the baby-soft hair, the loaf-size black nose, and the muscular mountain of hump. Then, before anyone noticed, the cosmic clock suddenly ran out of sand, and the gods quickly slapped a donkey butt onto the unfinished rear of the buffalo before the blaze of creation fizzled out, saying, "This'll just have to do..."

As I was saying, bison are, at best, ungainly, but they were far from their best on that day. Behind them stretched months of near starvation and relentless cold. Here at the crossroads of the seasons, their bodies stood in mute testament to the receding winter. The fat that had surrounded them last fall was long gone, and they were little more than a herd of ambulatory broomsticks with huge hides thrown over them.

Watching them, I was struck with humility for what they had endured. It was a sobering moment. That is, until one of the bison — a young male — heaved his bulk up onto a picnic table. As if that feat were not remarkable enough in itself, the bison suddenly began leaping about, doing an amazing performance of the tarantella. His comrades ignored him for as long as possible, but one by one they looked up and glanced his way.

Some stared at him. No one joined in. Like company at a formal dinner party where one guest suddenly arrives in cutoffs and a Hawaiian shirt, the surrounding buffalo looked as though they would have liked to raise their noses high in the air and sniff disgustedly. But their heads don't quite work that way, so they were limited to simple stares and snorts.

For a minute or two, the dancing bison succumbed to his inner child and clattered robustly on the table. I was thinking he could give the Lord of the Dance a run for his clogs. Then, panting, the bison jumped from the table and crashed into a nearby neighbor, who grunted indignantly and sideswiped him with her horns. Unfazed, the young bull trotted tail up through the unappreciative crowd. Perhaps because of his charisma or his infectious sense of abandon, he somehow gathered a small cadre of participants, and other bison began a halfhearted jig through the rest of the bemused herd.

The bison were at the weakest they would be all year, their energy depleted and their stomachs hollow. Yet some took a small spark of endurance and converted it into dance and levity. Behind my tree blind, I couldn't help shaking my head at the absurd scene I was privy to.

Spring

I'd been knocked out of my solemn musings on the tribulations of winter by a chorus line of bison that refused to take my earnest compassion for them seriously.

What is it about spring that would entice nature to spend her last handful of winter resources on a silly, cavorting dance? Leaning against the tree, I felt a riffle of energy, like a tiny fingerling trout coursing upstream along my backbone. It had been many years since I played for the sheer joy and abandon of it, many years since spring grabbed me in that way.

When I was little, play was something I did with my large family of stuffed animals or with a pile of sticks I would stack over and over again to create a small cabin. I recalled an image of myself bent over a gutter full of water, pretending it was a wild river. Sometimes, I would wrap myself in one of my grandmother's flimsy scarves and dance like I was a fairy princess or Thumbelina or a gypsy queen, or all three at once.

The last buffalo trotted away from the picnic area, waving her donkey tail jauntily behind her just because she could. The tip of her tail flounced like a small brush, scribbling a secret message for me in the blue air: *Play is where dreams are born*. Stepping out from behind the tree, I placed my feet carefully, thoughtfully, into the notched moons of her hoofprints. It came to me abruptly, in a trance of recognition, that my childhood play had become the reality of my life.

I lived in a pile of sticks — my log cabin. And my family of toy animals — even the bat and the chimpanzee — had come to me in their living forms over the years. The rivers I loved were no longer limited by gutters and storm drains. The fairy dancer had had her day, also. When I was diagnosed with cancer, the first thing I did — completely beyond my understanding at the time — was to buy a pair of ballet toe shoes and twirl around my small apartment like Thumbelina or the gypsy queen. In truth, I have played my way into life and healing.

My friend's husband played baseball all his young years and turned his play into a career, collecting and selling sports memorabilia. My former boss took up the piano and tap dancing when she was in her fifties because she had never had a chance to play at these things in her younger days. Another man I know turned his love of creek-side wandering and play into a career as a naturalist. Best at combining work and play, though, are my dogs, who never seem to distinguish between the two. And now there were these buffalo dancers.

Whether our play ever turns into work is not really the point. The point is to play, because otters, crows, bears, and bison tell us it is worth the doing. In the evolutionary process, only what works survives. Millions of years of play add up to a powerful advertisement for its efficacy. Frolic and you will be in good company.

Spring exacts this of us. She insists that we be filled up with an energy so boundless that it spills over in fantastical ways. I suppose buffalo table-dance because they just can't *not*. All that energy has to go somewhere, and why not to some brilliant, catalyzing silliness? Sometime very soon, I promised myself, I would tap-dance on a picnic table.

ON CONTAINMENT
Circlesong

*Birds make their nest in circles, for theirs is the
same religion as ours.*

— BLACK ELK

I NOTICED A MOVEMENT out of the corner of my eye,
and my brain registered "bullet-shaped bird body." All
the hairs rose up on my arms in sudden excitement.
Meadowlark! The first of the season! Sure enough, there
he was on the corner fence rail in all his courting colors,
his breast the color of a ripe lemon and the black half-
moon under his chin shining like a raven's beak. Before

I could get up out of my chair, he flung his head back and began a rippling, flutelike tune that sent shivers down my back. I have heard the old tales that birdsong wakes up the plant kingdom and calls the grass out of the ground and the new leaves out of the trees. Surely, the meadowlark sings up the daffodils.

By the time I got to my room upstairs and shoved open the window to let in his music, a fresh curtain of new snow had started falling again. Through white flakes big as quarters, I could see the meadowlark still singing his heart out. Somewhere out there, he would find the perfect spot for his nest — a small, rounded bowl made in the soil — and someone to share it.

The first robins had visited my yard two days earlier, when the ground was frozen hard and worms were locked beneath it. I set out apple halves, and the robins picked them clean, leaving the skins behind like red china cups. All this bird energy got me thinking about yet another cup — a fragile container from a March not long past, when I had sold my house and moved to a small, tired cabin. It was a time much like the current one, when the receding snows left mud in their wake — that deep, boglike muck that sucks off shoes and swallows them whole.

I was sorrowing then for what I had left behind: a beautiful big house and barn, and a family of animals who could not make the journey to this new, very cramped place. The weather outside had said, *Stay indoors. Rest. No point in fighting the mud and the cold*. And so I did. I unpacked slowly, pondering the contents of each box as I put my life on shelves, in drawers, in closets. No lark sang in the trees on that cold day. My own sound was not a song, then, but a sigh. I'd been sighing a lot — big, deep sighs you pull up from the belly.

Arrow had whined at the door and looked at me over her shoulder. Distracted for a moment from my melancholy reverie, I'd put on my purple barn jacket — which reminded me that I no longer had a barn — and stepped outside. Arrow charged past me like a rocket, bounding through the wet snow. Immediately, she put her nose to the ground and began sniffing, circling in an inward spiral until she found the exact place to roll, her hairy feet pointing skyward and her body wiggling.

Watching her, I'd nearly tripped on an empty robin's nest that had fallen from its perch above the front porch light. It was a sodden blob there on the porch, but it was easy to see that some bird had spent a lot of time constructing it. Leaving Arrow to her romp, I carried the nest into the house and put it on the kitchen counter, where I could look at it more closely. There was something almost meditative in the way the twigs leaked brown water in a Rorschach shape across the Formica.

Why Buffalo Dance

Through a complex weaving of sticks and grass, the robin had interlaced threads of colorful horsehair. To cushion the center of the nest, she had collected soft yellow grasses and pressed them up against the nest's mud lining. My eyes took in the shape of the nest itself: a near perfect bowl. A magic circle cast in twigs and mud, universal symbol of union, infinity, and cosmic order.

I imagined the robin creating this little masterpiece, carrying in her beak strands of horsehair, twigs, and finally, tiny mouthfuls of wet mud. Round and round her body would have turned, like a potter's hands at a wheel, molding an exquisitely thin chalice of clay to line her nest. The potter's wheel is a circle, too — a circle that creates by motion.

The Lakota word for life is *taku sk'an sk'an* — something in motion, something moving. Life: a thing that moves and yet is always contained, as a circle is always contained. This soggy nest could tell a rich story about life, circles, and movement. I knew that if I put the nest back above the porch light, there was a good chance the robins would return and build a fresh one on top of it, using the old to help fashion something new.

Arrow greeted me at the front door, bouncing excitedly as I returned the nest to its place above the light. I set the nest back gently, as one would place the grail — another kind of nest, another kind of circular container.

Then I hurried back inside, leaving my wet shoes at the door, aware that I had a nest of my own to create.

Mourning is an autumn task, the unfolding of every edge of what was, so that it can be laid flat and swept clean. And I had been mourning and sweeping long past the season for it. Spring asks something different of the hands that hold the broom. It whispers to them to come together in the form of a cup, something with soft, rounded sides that can contain the new life about to spill into them.

Spring dreams are like blue robin's eggs, like round seeds. Uncontained, they will roll, spin, drop, scatter, or shatter. My sister Teresa tells me, "Spring is the season for flying by the seat of your pants, you know; but if you lay your eggs in midair, they won't hatch. You need to have done the winter work of making yourself a strong container for the new beginnings of spring. How do you do that? It's different for each person, like each nest is different."

Some people build their nests with good food and exercise, some with spiritual practices, reading, deep conversation with friends, service to the community, a stable and secure home, long, reflective walks, or satisfying work. I built my own nest that spring by cleaning, tidying, and personalizing the little cabin until it became a friendly, comforting space that would ground me in a new life. I hung bird feeders, collected driftwood and circled the porch with it, grew a planterful of pansies, and made a fire pit outside where friends and I would roast marshmallows and talk during the long evenings.

That cabin was six years behind me now, and my mind returned to the present and to fresh snow whirling in spiral patterns outside as the meadowlark continued to sing. I thought about the unforeseen treasures of life that had been hatched in that little cabin where I lived for only six months, including a noisy clutch of young robins above the porch light. This spring, I was ready with a settled home and a settled heart to enfold whatever round seeds spring would roll my way. *Taku sk'an sk'an* — I would contain the precious, rollicking motion of life and not let it scatter.

ON THE TRICKSTER
April Fool

Trickster is a creator, a transformer, a joker, a truth-teller, a destroyer.... Trickster fuzzes the lines between...wisdom and stupidity.... Trickster tells us the truth about ourselves.

— THUNDERSPUD OF DRAGONFHAIN

A DRY CREEK BED MEANDERED around the back of the garden shed. Soon the waters would begin to flow as the spring runoff began, and the creek would be full of gurgling water and a fish or two. For the time being, the creek stones were gray and dry, many of them covered with the brown, chalky remains of last summer's algae. Fox tracks crisscrossed the silt at the creek bed's edge, and I wondered what it would be like when the water came and this creek began talking each day with the voice of rushing liquid over stone.

In the mountains, spring comes late and leaves early. I waited impatiently for the ice to melt and for the land to take on the look of summer. I hurried my own life along in the same way, wanting to rush it through the dark days, the between times. In this part of the Rockies, we call the time between tourist visits the "shoulder season." The town seems to suspend its breath between the avalanche of summer and winter visitors.

I was in my own shoulder season and was wishing it were over. This time-between felt like nothing-time. A time when I felt anxious, lost, quick-tempered, and out of sorts. My inner cry was the Olympic motto, "Let the games begin!" However, in the pause between winter and spring, it seemed to me that no one was ready to play.

But all around me, animals were telling me that the games were already in high gear. Everywhere, birds were flying with grass and sticks in their mouths. Geese sat on eggs in secret nests by the river. I knew this because I had found the remains of an egg in one of the dry, side channels of the river the last evening I walked the dogs. It was a section about the size of my hand, curved like a half-moon, hard as a shard of porcelain, and smeared with a brilliant blaze of yellow yoke on the inner rim.

Spring

I stood at the creek on dry stones, waiting for signs that were already whirling around me like universes, unnoticed. Why is it that I search for the big, flashy omens? The river and creeks were speaking of spring, but not in brassy greens and burbling water torrents. At least not yet. The voice was gray, soft, wet, stark, and chilled. But it was a voice that spoke insistently to the animals, who listened to these colors and sounds. The birds were already playing at spring, at new beginnings, while I looked for the bolder, quaking signs that I relied on. Spring had already begun, whether I'd heard it or not.

April Fools' Day had arrived, the day of Coyote, the trickster spirit of Native American tradition, the holy fool who turns the order of the universe upside down and finds wisdom in the absurd. In the back-and-forth dances of winter-spring, I'd certainly felt my own sense of absurdity. Next to my porch was a garden rake I'd taken out two weeks earlier, with the fantasy of cleaning out all the dead winter grasses in the tree beds. Within an hour of unburying the rake, I watched the winds rise to thirty-five miles an hour and the temperature fall to below twenty degrees. Now, the rake sat in five inches of icy snow and slush.

Back in winter mode, I exchanged my rubber boots for wool-lined mukluks, but by noon I was sloshing through snowmelt puddles downtown with very wet, cold feet. Coyote giggles. Is it winter or isn't it? Should I put away my down jackets or not? Time to ice-skate or time to swim?

In my own seasonal turnings, I always struggle during this time that encompasses the end of many things and the not-quite-blossoming of others. The between-times of life are believed to be profound times of inner processing, reconciliation, and insight. Yet there is something about limbo — no matter how useful a time it is — that is utterly unappealing. Surviving such times requires drastic measures, like a good dose of humor and absurdity. It is no surprise that April Fools' Day, a holiday dedicated to exactly this kind of energy, is a springtime event. I think Coyote planned it that way.

The other morning a neighbor came by to deliver a newspaper, and as he left he said, "Something pooped on your mat outside..." I went out to look and found a ropy pile of lumpy, hair-filled droppings deposited on the outer edge of Arrow's dog bed. Too big for a cat. Certainly not Arrow's signature calling card. Too big for a fox. But just right for Coyote.

I shoveled the poop pile off the porch and went upstairs and drew Coyote from my deck of Animal Cards: "Explore the present chaos. See life's humor.... Welcome the unexpected."

ON THE TRUE NAME OF THINGS
Horsehair Callings

Ged sighed sometimes, but he did not complain. He saw that in this dusty and fathomless matter of learning the true name of each place, thing and being, the power he wanted lay like a jewel at the bottom of a dry well. For magic consists in this, the true naming of a thing.

— URSULA K. LE GUIN, *A WIZARD OF EARTHSEA*

NO MATTER HOW HARD THE SNOW TRIED to reblanket the valley, the sun defied it. Just the length of the days alone was too much now for the spring blizzards, and the white flakes melted away like vanilla ice cream on a hot brownie. Many birds had returned to the valley: bluebirds, osprey, sandhill cranes, kestrels, and red-winged blackbirds.

Why Buffalo Dance

Ground squirrels were awake at long last, whistling in the grass across the road while they excavated fresh new tunnels, piling up dirt mounds everywhere. Sage grouse performed their mating dances on the airport runway. Owlets were hatching, along with eaglets, goslings, and ravens. Grizzly bears again roamed the forests, and deer gathered along the highway in groups, moving off to who-knows-where for the summer.

Despite the signs of the season rampant in the animal world, there was only the briefest suggestion of leaves on the trees, and the wind could still be brutal. The snow sat like white ponds in areas where the shadows remained heavy, and the river sat locked up in ice. I felt impatience rising in me like mercury in a thermometer and wondered if I would see a warm day ever again. I don't mind huddling by a fire or bundling up in winter clothes so thick I look like a walking salami. But I started to mind when it felt like winter was never coming to an end. For days, I'd been feeling fidgety and restless.

I grabbed my binoculars and took the dogs for their first walk of many we would take that day. Mist hung like a cloud all along the river bottom and swirled around the trees like cold smoke. Strongheart turned his face to the icy breeze and squinted his eyes. His cheeks puffed up as he sucked in great, deep breaths, nose held high, ears flapping. Arrow's head was in a hole, her long collie snout poking and snuffling.

In summer, it's easy to locate Strongheart when he is outside, because he's the size and color of a polar bear. Arrow — all brown and feathery-haired — looks like a bush and becomes invisible at around five yards' distance. In winter, the table turns, and Strongheart can vanish in front of your nose in an instant. A few nights earlier in the twilight, I mistook Arrow for a brown doormat and fell over her on my way to the shed.

Strongheart stopped to offer a quiet woof at the mare in my neighbor's corral, and I slowed to watch a magpie hopping down her back. Every now and again, the magpie stopped to pick at something on the horse's spine. I fished out my binoculars to watch and discovered that the bird was pulling out tufts of dead winter fur with his beak. He moved down to the horse's broad rump and yanked out a few strands of tail hair. With his mouth completely full, he hopped back up to the mare's shoulder and took the hair bundle in his feet. Fluttering his wings for balance as the horse shifted, he began carefully pulling the strands of hair into an untangled, well-organized swath of bunting with his beak. When he had arranged the materials to his liking, he flew off and dove into a massive pile of jumbled sticks stacked two feet high in an overgrown serviceberry bush. It was

his nest, a creation I have dubbed "architecture-with-out-borders."

Unlike me, the magpie was not the least bit deterred by the lack of greenery. He knew that spring was already here, and that the merest suggestion of green growth and fertile eggs was as good as a reality. *Auwk-auwk-auwk!* His magpie voice rattled like an electric drill boring through brick. In an instant, he was on his way back to the mare, who must have loved the scratchy feel of his toes in her greasy winter coat. I caught the glance of the magpie's black, beaded eye as he flew past: *Get your house in order*, he admonished me. *The growing time is here!*

Growing time. I lowered my binoculars with a laugh of recognition. The anxiousness coursing through me: how easy it was to label it impatience. I fussed and fidgeted and walked the dogs four times a day and called it frustration with the weather, while the magpie filled his mouth with hair and named for me the thing that had really taken over my body and my emotions.

Like sap coursing up a tree trunk, spring was running through me. Each year, I forget that spring in the Rockies is something that is always coming and that never quite arrives, because when it does arrive, it's called summer. Just when the weather starts to mellow and the cottonwoods explode with *actual green leaves!* — poof! It is June. From March to late May, I wander around twitching, waiting, grousing, and *this* is spring.

In a geography where spring only hints at itself, it is easy to feel the restless urgency characteristic of this season. Perhaps in the East, where magnolias bloom and warm days lull the senses, spring fever is a reality. But not here. In this land, we all have to adjust to the agitating itch of our own sap rising. We can stick a grimace on our faces and twitch around like we have ants in our underwear, or we can take a cue from Magpie, who harnesses the very same energy and channels it into preparation.

Impatience. Preparation. I rolled the two words around on my tongue. They tasted completely different, one bitter, the other refreshingly tart. Energy moves in the direction we name and takes on that flavor, good or ill. Preparation. Impatience. One name gathers the energy. The other scatters it. It was time to get my house in order. I had all the restless energy of spring to put to the task the minute I called it by its right name.

ON NEW BEGINNINGS

Fawning

What is this talked-of mystery of birth
But being mounted bareback on the earth?

— ROBERT FROST

I USED TO TAKE IN ORPHANED FAWNS in spring. Some of them came to me because their mothers had been struck by cars. Some had been injured by dogs. Too many were picked up by well-meaning people who found them in the forest alone and mistakenly assumed they had been abandoned. Deer will leave their young alone for hours to avoid bringing predatory attention to them. While the mothers are away, the fawns will lie motionless and perfectly camouflaged in the grasses and leaves.

One unusually warm spring night in May, I waited by the door for the arrival of an orphaned fawn. When the officer showed up with the infant in a cardboard cat carrier, the story he told me is one I'd never heard before and doubted I'd ever hear again. A woman driving home in the early dark of the evening turned the corner to her garage and startled a doe curled up in the gravel in front of the garage doors. In the glare of the headlights, she saw the doe leap to her feet, bewildered, and spring off into the trees.

The woman said that, in the confusion, it looked to her as though the doe had tossed a paper lunch sack onto the driveway before she bolted. Stepping out of her car to inspect the bundle, the woman found a struggling fawn encased in a ruptured sack of birth membrane. Evidently, the doe had been in the process of giving birth when the woman drove up and was unable to forestall the event for even a few more seconds.

The woman rushed to the house, made a few phone calls, put the car away, and waited to see if the doe would return. She didn't. I thanked the officer for taking the time to drive the fawn to my cabin, and then shut the door behind me, expecting it would be a long time before I saw my bed that evening.

The dogs were intensely curious, having smelled this aroma before. They snuffled around the box while I put some infant formula on the stove to heat. The old stove of mine, a 1952 Wedgewood enamel-and-chrome job, had heated up countless bottles of formula over the decades and had been the makeshift nest site for innumerable baby birds. The pilot light kept the stovetop and oven warm, making it the perfect staging area for wildlife foundlings.

From house to house, I'd lugged the stove along with me, always the heaviest and worst piece to move of anything I've owned or likely will own. Thanks to the Internet, I'd been able to find extra parts when I needed them to keep the Wedgewood running. The stove was the center of any home I found myself in, like the hearth and heart of old Irish cottages. Anything I cooked on its burners was particularly tasty and comforting, or so it seemed to me.

While the formula heated, I took a moment to open the cat carrier and meet my newest houseguest. The fawn curled almost invisibly at the bottom of the carton. She was dry now, but in the dim lamplight I could make out the curls in her sweet-smelling coat. No one had licked her clean, and the birth fluids had plastered her fur like a coating of hairspray.

The dogs settled down a few feet away when I told

them to, and I lifted the tiny fawn out of the box. She was the size of a half-grown kitten and felt like a cuttlebone in my hand, all her angles sharp and narrow. Her umbilical cord hung like a wet spaghetti noodle. The light caught the shimmering white spots on her pelt, and her small feet were still covered with a white membrane of spongy flesh — slippers, they are called — designed to keep her from perforating her mother's womb. I tried to stand her up, but her limbs were like rubber and she collapsed instinctively into a loose pile. When she flattened her head against the carpet, I noticed her eyes for the first time. They were wide and stunned. The head that held those eyes looked impossibly small for the job, like a tiny galaxy attempting to hold two oversize planets.

Ringed with long, black lashes and Egyptian-style eyeliner, the orphan's eyes would have been a work of art even had they not contained the miracle of sight. But I knew these eyes could see, because they darted around the room now and then, coming back to rest in a vacant, bottomless stare. Her expression was not sad, just stunned. I'd seen that look before in the eyes of many newborns, from chicks to colts. I suspected I came into the world with a similar expression on my own face.

The bottle was warm, and I imagined that, in the absence of her mother's tongue, it was the bottle that would coax her into her new life here on earth. I sprinkled some of the formula on my finger and dabbed it on her lips, using a soft, stroking motion on her mouth to persuade her. All the while I spoke in soft, baby tones or hummed a cradle song. Finally, her pink tongue snaked out and licked the milk off her nose. She licked again, and a light switched on in her eyes.

I held her up in the crook of my arm and eased the rubber lamb's nipple into her mouth. Her tongue popped out and wrapped around the bottle the way a paper liner encircles an ice cream cone. In the next instant, she was sucking, her lower lip moving forward and back, the milk beginning to make fizzing sounds in the bottle as the suction took hold. She blinked while she drank, her long lashes fluttering like maiden-fly wings.

When she finished, she spit the nipple out and twitched her ears, taking a long look around the room. This time, she found strength in her legs and stood wobbly but balanced, looking this way and that, flipping her ears back and forward. I hurried to the kitchen for a warm washcloth and a soft brush to freshen her fur. The rubbing seemed to invigorate her, and she tossed her head and put a determined foot forward. Four or five inquisitive steps were all she managed before pulling her legs beneath her and sinking back into a folded heap with her chin hugging her side. It was enough activity for one hour. I lifted her carefully and set her on a blanket by the heating stove.

The dogs remained curious but respectful. Arrow was dying to sniff her all over, but I knew she would keep her distance until I let her know it was okay to go forward. And while I wanted to let Arrow and Strongheart make friends with her, I didn't. This small fawn came into the world with the odds stacked against her. Already, she was missing both a mother and a good dose of colostrum. An affinity for dogs would just about cinch her fate.

While I iodined her umbilical cord and made a bed for the fawn in my closet, I couldn't help but think of the remarkable circumstances of her birth. She didn't land on earth; she dropped here from four feet up, crashing with an unceremonious thud onto cold gravel.

Years ago when I raised donkeys, I attended many of their night births. One of my jennies, SiSi, always had a rough time of it, pushing herself to the point of exhaustion before her foal would finally arrive. I remember one night sitting spread legged at the back end of SiSi, encouraging her while she struggled to expel her foal. It seemed that we were stuck forever in that moment when the nose protrudes but nothing else happens. Then, suddenly, a whole package of legs and ears and warm water shot into my lap. I laughed out loud at the suddenness of

it and at the overwhelming sense of release I felt, sitting there in a flood of water and birth tissue.

Like the unexpected arrivals of the fawn and my donkey baby, there comes a moment when life bursts out, unstoppable, in a wet, hot rush of opportunity. Grace willing, nature sends appropriate midwives to tend to the new life: soft grass, silence, gentle hands, a ready and comforting tongue. But sometimes, the birth of something hot, fresh, and new arrives with a startling, cold flight onto hard gravel.

Little comes to us in life in the way we expect. Most of the big things that shift our courses are never anticipated at all, and suddenly there we are, looking around with stunned eyes and little idea of which way to steer next. Dreams germinate into opportunities, and opportunities deliver themselves, sometimes on welcoming straw, sometimes on a cold driveway.

No matter which, when the time comes there is no saying, "Oh let's just wait a minute longer…" If we are wise, we will scurry to make the very best of the opportunity we're given. Spring gives us the gift of new prospects. And it carries another gift as well. Like winter, spring bestows its own kind of magic. Who would have thought the fawn would be born on a driveway and abandoned? More amazingly, who would have thought that, even so, there would be arms waiting for her? As

uncontrollable as spring is, there is an equal, matching mystery to help us make the most of it.

I looked at the sleeping fawn gleaming in the firelight and wished she could have arrived gently to the kisses of starlight and welcoming soil. But when a thing is ready to be born, it arrives on its own heavenly timetable. I could not know then that she would be a lucky one, reaching adulthood and freedom with the help of many hands. So, for that night, I simply blessed the grace that had brought her to my door, and determined — with the help of the season — to make the very best of it.

ON THE LAW OF ATTRACTION

The Magpies and the Weasel

Go to a place in nature that attracts you.... Ask this area for permission for you to be there. Doing this increases your sensitivity to the area. Ask if this place will help you learn from it. Look for adverse signals of danger such as thorns, bees, cliff faces. If the area still feels attractive, or becomes more attractive, you have gained its consent to be there.

— MICHAEL COHEN

A STEADY STREAM OF MAGPIES winged back and forth over my head like stunt planes on a popular flight path. The air was crisp as pears, and a small breeze ruffled the tips of new grass. Looking through my binoculars, I saw that the magpies were all moving to and from a large cottonwood tree at the edge of a stream channel, so I veered off in that direction with the dogs, slightly changing the course of our usual pasture walk.

Why Buffalo Dance

Still leafless, the cottonwood was dressed this morning in bird chatter that grew louder as I came nearer. Not wanting to disturb the magpies from whatever had grabbed their interest, I sat on the ground and raised the binoculars again.

Cottonwood trees are raggedy things, bearded with dense tangles of twigs sprouting from their lower trunks. When they grow in stands, they seem to spring up from a brush pile of their own making. Moving my eyes up the trunk of the tree, I saw a big bundle of interlocking sticks and twigs that was clearly not growing there. It was the old nest of a red-tailed hawk couple who had raised babies there the previous spring. Like impatient shoppers waiting in line for opening day at the mall, the magpies flapped and fussed side by side in the limbs nearby. One or two of them at a time stepped forward to the nest, closely inspected the huge mound of jumbled sticks, twigs, and grass, and eventually made their selection.

Sometimes, they chose twigs from the bottom of the pile and had to yank and tug at their prizes to claim them. Other magpies squawked encouragement. Why is it that you always have to dig to get at the good stuff? As soon as the shoppers flew off with their trophies, other magpies stepped forward to peruse the merchandise.

I could see from the disarray of the nest that magpies had been visiting this windfall for days. The birds seemed to have decided that this was a closeout sale and everything must go. The hawk nest was slowly being recycled into something entirely new — magpie nests. The dual nature of the magpies' ingenuity delighted me, and if I'd had a hat, I would have tipped it to them. By carting twigs off from the hawk nest, the birds were both assembling new homes for themselves and demolishing the home of an adversary.

When the hawks returned, they would have to start building from scratch. The magpies made it just a little more difficult for the hawks to settle into the neighborhood. Perhaps the raptors would move on to a more hospitable location.

Meanwhile, I realized that my behind was cold and wet from sitting on the grass, and I'd inadvertently stuck my feet into a patch of the tiny burrs that engulf your socks, then stab your ankles. Clearly, I was not listening when I sat down. If I'd had my inner ears tuned, I'd have chosen a more welcoming spot, but the magpie activity had momentarily deafened me. The hawk wasn't the only one being invited to move on that morning. The cold and the burrs extended their invitation to me to find someplace better to sit, someplace more *attractive*.

The ecopsychologist Michael Cohen has made a life's work of reconnecting people with nature and believes that one of the most important laws we have forgotten about the earth is the Law of Attraction and Consent. For life to thrive — not merely hang on but thrive and expand — Cohen believes it needs the consent, or welcome, of its surroundings. We recognize this natural sensation of consent in our bodies, and we are attracted to places and people who welcome us. In the presence of such people and places, we thrive. Cohen believes that animals and plants feel this sense in their own unique ways, and this sense moves all of life forward into health and well-being.

If I'd followed this law that morning, I'd have had a dry behind, and I couldn't help but think of the weasel who lived in my neighbor's yard. He was a beautiful little creature with black button eyes and a soft yellow crescent moon under his chin. In winter, he would turn completely white except for a black swish like a paintbrush at the tip of his tail. It's hard to believe that anything that cute could be so fierce. After the weasel moved in, an entire colony of ground squirrels moved out, and my neighbor was delighted. His yard was no longer attractive to rodents of any kind.

Finding a dry rock to sit on, I began pulling the resistant burrs from my socks and shoelaces. The magpies were still at it, loudly. I remembered a phrase from my younger years: the Law of Attraction. I thought it meant that, the more attractive you were, the more successful you'd be. Not until I stumbled upon Cohen's work did I consider attraction to be something you needed to follow, not just something you needed to exude.

Last year, a colony of sunflowers sprouted beneath the feeders in the front of the cabin. Another stand sprung up out back. The cabin faces east, and the cluster of sunflowers out front was bathed in morning sun all summer. Out back, the patch of sunflowers faced west, into the hottest and most brilliant sunlight of the day, every day. This small group stood above a mound of pebbles in their own little rock garden. The flowers out front competed for space with dense grass and seedling aspens. By the end of summer, when the sunflower plants began to blossom, there were hardly any left to bloom out front. But the backyard stand was dazzling, with flower heads so full and heavy that many of them eventually toppled over.

The only difference between the two patches of sunflowers was that the flowers out back had been given full *consent to be*. They had by providence settled in a more welcoming environment. No grasses fought them for space and food, the pebbles warmed them, and the sun was especially generous to them. Everything in their environment welcomed them there and supported them.

The Law of Attraction applies to more than sunflowers. For several years, I lived on a beautiful island in the Northwest. I loved the place, but oddly enough, the place didn't love me. Every job I was offered dried up and blew away for one reason or another, every new friend I made moved somewhere else, and the tiny church I attended closed its doors. For three years, I looked for any way I could find into that community but never found one. Nothing welcomed me. Nothing consented generously to my being there. Eventually, I moved away and quickly found all the things that had so eluded me on the island of my dreams. There have been other dreams that I have nurtured, but which never found the right place or time to grow, no matter how earnestly I tended them.

I've had intimate relationships in which I tried to force my ideas into our small community of two, never thinking to ask for consent first and never gaining the welcoming warmth that consent brings. Eventually, feeling no attraction to remain, I moved on or my partner moved on. When I was stricken with cancer, there were the rare, blessed few who said to me, "Would you like to hear my ideas about this?" or "Can you talk to me about dying?" Their sensitivity allowed me the option to consent to the conversation or decline. I felt welcomed by their consideration for my circumstances and safe enough with these people to share.

When we were small, we were told to say "please"

and "thank you." Maybe it was one of the most important lessons we were taught. Our parents' parents' parents — to the tenth power — understood that we lived
in a world where simple consideration had profound
value. Were we welcome? Did we know how to welcome others? Before barging into circumstances, did we
have the good sense to ask permission? Before we offered
our advice to a friend, did we know enough to seek their
consent first? Did we know what "no" meant? Wars
have been started over issues of blundering and rude-
ness. "Please" and "thank you" are still valuable lessons
of relationship and peace.

My socks were free of burrs, and my pants nearly
dry, but I was thirsty, and the idea of my teakettle sitting
on the stove was growing very attractive to me, so I
called the dogs and we headed back home. Overhead,
I heard the taffeta rustling of feathers, and a magpie
winged past with a long twig in his beak. I hoped he had
found a good, inviting place to put it.

Moments later, when I rounded the corner of my
garden shed, I ran into the magpie again. I recognized
him by the twig he still held in his beak. In the thick willows alongside the shed, near a platform feeder where
I put cat food and cheese for the crows and magpies, I
saw the skeleton outline of a new nest. It would be as big
and dense as a beehive before long. Pivoting his head

from side to side, the magpie worked the twig skillfully between the dense willow branches and wove his construction timber into his new springtime masterpiece. I told him he was welcome there, and that, as a matter of fact, he couldn't have chosen a more attractive spot.

ON GREENING
A Tail of Burrs

If I keep a green bough in my heart, then the singing bird will come.

— CHINESE PROVERB

A FAT ROBIN NESTED on the log butt high above my living room window. She always sat facing east, and I could see her shining eye and earnest face when I sat on the front porch. Killdeers had been mating on the dirt road, perched on top of each other like tiny gymnasts. Mourning doves came in a flock to the back pasture every morning and evening, their beautiful peach-beige bodies shimmering in the rising and setting suns.

Why Buffalo Dance

The leaves of the arrowleaf balsamroot rose out of the ground like a buried army of twisting lance heads. Only days before, I had watched a young vole racing among their short green stalks looking desperately for a hole to hide himself in. He didn't find any that suited him while I was watching, although he stuck his head in more than one. Fussy guy. I wondered how long he would survive in a pasture overseen by nesting owls and hawks.

All along the faces of the hillsides, the aspens had budded. Some still displayed their lanternlike catkins swaying like party decorations in the spring winds. I looked expectantly at the cottonwood trees; but cottonwoods keep their spring exuberance to themselves, and they still looked as dry and spent as they had all winter. They reminded me of late arrivals at a party. They would make a spectacular, grand, green entrance when they finally decided to turn out, which was always later than I expected.

Everywhere, birds were sitting, sitting, sitting with fixed and determined stares. Under them all sat clutches of eggs or clutches of babies. Canada geese strolled along shorelines, with goslings lined up behind them like strings of fuzzy pearls. Ravens scouted for nests of tiny fledglings to cart off and feed to their own ravenous young if parent birds were not quick or strong enough in defending their own nests.

Spring

It was time for coyote pups to begin wobbling out of their dens. Bison, deer, and a few early elk had delivered their young already. But this month, it was not the hot pink of newly hatched birds or the spotted pelts of infant elk, the red coats of baby bison or the shrub-colored fur of coyote young, that dominated the season. The color of the month was green. Green in all its shades and shadows and tongues. Spiraling shoots of young grass, fattening leaves, and the unfurling heads of wildflowers, all were singing the music of vitality, fertility, vigor, and renewal.

I walked Arrow up the canyon along carpets of budding clover, vetch, and grass and lamented as her collie coat — just like Velcro — caught hold of every sticky burr that had been left beneath the winter's snow. She put her nose down a fresh vole hole, snorted vigorously, and, when she pulled back her chin, was studded with dozens of spiky barbs as small as pinheads. She has always been nature's traveling seed collector, designed to cart seeds and burrs vast distances over plains, creeks, sidewalks, and pastures each fall and spring, and she does a fine job of it.

So fine, in fact, that I walked armed with a doggie comb and brush — trail tools as vital as my water bottle and snack bag. When we sat down for lunch, I brought out the comb and got to work, first snaking the wire teeth down her back and along her flanks. She groaned and sighed and fell backward into my lap, all eighty pounds of her, while I raked out burrs as big as my thumb and as small as a dot of sand. Her plume tail was the prime collection zone, a veritable dust wand for stickery stuff.

The round burrs reminded me of last year's old dreams, blackened and soggy from a winter's worth of dark and cold and snow, now coated with a tangle of tail hair. I held a clump of them in my fingers and said, "This is the idea I had about traveling to the coast for the winter, before I ran out of funds to do it. Here is the dream of baking sourdough bread that I never pursued, even once. And this big fat cactuslike burr" — I held it out to Arrow — "this is the romance that never materialized last Christmas, or the previous Christmas, or the Christmas before that."

When I dropped these weed pods onto the carpet of green grass under me, the tender blades reached out like fingers and pulled them down under and away, hastening to wipe out my memories of what never was. The grasses were about what is; and what is, is greenness and freshness and the energy of becoming. The time for these spent burrs was all done for the time being. Arrow sniffed the breeze. It was cool and tangy with the scent of running snowmelt and sun on granite.

Spring

All around me, the forest floor sent up green messengers of passion and sent down threadlike roots to anchor the new foliage. I rubbed my hands together and wiped away barbs of the old weed heads I'd held, reminding myself that I, too, needed to begin sending down new, tentative roots of my own to steady my newborn dreams and hopes.

On such a day, dreams were quickening in me, responding helplessly to all the wild and insistent greening all around and above. How could the heart — whose color is often represented symbolically as green — not send up new shoots right alongside the grasses and the chokecherry leaves? Is there any better season for it?

There comes a time when green enters your life — no matter what season it really is outside. The old moldered stuff has to go then, even if you aren't quite ready to shake it off when it sticks valiantly to your coat ("I wanted that romance. I wanted to bake good bread and have it scent the kitchen when there was snow outside..."). There is a reason when seeds — like certain dreams — don't take root. Not everything can grow. And that which doesn't becomes the soil containing all that is blessed enough to send up a shoot. Whether the cause was timing, grace, or mystery, the shriveled burrs I'd held in my hand were not meant to be anything else this time around.

Why Buffalo Dance

It wasn't long before I had little piles of stickers and dog hair encircling me. Arrow was tired of the salon job and struggled to get up and away. By the time we returned home, I knew, I could sit her down and start brushing out burrs all over again, but for the rest of that day I dreamed about green, instead.

SUMMER

SUMMER

South Wind, all that you are —
Season of summer, house of red-blazing heat, noontime
　　of the day, sun at its most brilliant.
Dwelling place of the coyote and the rabbit.
Guardian of the young.
Place of growth, ripening, warmth, and sharing.
The growing time of our garden, the joy of flowers, and
　　the warm fire of love and friendship.
Time of weeding, tending, and feeding the dreams and
　　possibilities birthed in spring.
Guide us through this time of nurturing dreams and
　　opportunities
Into our fullest, ripest selves.
Help us to use these radiant and fiery energies of the
　　season in a good way,
Putting our effort into things that enrich life rather than
　　demolish it.
May the seeds we have sprouted grow strong and tall,
　　and may we learn to distinguish
The healthy plants from those that are weak or sickly
　　and not meant to blossom.
Take us along riverbanks and forest edges, where we
　　may learn from
The fledging osprey, the ripening berries, and the
　　bounding elk calves.
Show us what your relatives know about maturity,
　　abundance, and flight.
South Wind, blow through us. Bring us your blessings
　　and your wisdom.

ON PULSE AND RHYTHM

Heart of the River

Best of all is it to preserve everything in a pure, still heart, and let there be for every pulse a thanksgiving and for every breath a song.

— KONRAD VON GESNER

SUMMER IS THE TIME OF MOVING WATER. The spring torrents are gone and the rivers have settled down to become emerald and azure. At the shallower places, you can even swim without turning blue. It is the perfect time for canoes and paddles and for lunches packed for friends. Along the shoreline, the tentative buds of spring have blossomed or leafed out by now or shriveled away.

Why Buffalo Dance

Big-eyed baby animals are sturdier now. The infants have thrived or become welcome food for predators.

Rounding the first bend of the river on a beautiful warm morning, my friend and I crossed the wake of an otter family. Their round heads cut through the water like a small flotilla of upturned teacups. When I caught sight of them, I couldn't help but blurt out exclamations. At the sound of my voice, the entire otter group turned our way and raised their heads for a better view.

To my surprise and delight, they swam back toward us, diving as they neared the canoe. A moment later, I could see them slipping through the water beneath us like a school of eels, trailing clusters of tiny white bubbles from their noses. When the bubbles reached the surface, they popped with a soft fizzing noise. For long moments I watched the otters like an excited toddler, with my mouth hanging open and my hands clenched. The young otters looked like miniature versions of their parents, just as quick, just as strongly muscled. Suddenly, in a choreographed burst of speed, they headed for the near shore, rocketed out of the water, and rolled and rolled their sleek bodies in the grass. They licked themselves, they licked each other, and they licked the grass. One of them shook off like a dog, spraying water over the entire gang, so the whole family had to start licking again.

Paddling farther downstream, we heard a crashing sound, as if a large concrete block had been dropped into the water. A short way off, an osprey flapped noisily in the current, then raised herself like a dripping phoenix into the air. In her talons, she held a good-size trout whose nose pointed backward. I knew she wouldn't stand for this, and so I set my paddle aside to watch her.

The osprey surged upward steep and fast. At a certain height, her feet relaxed and she dropped the trout, which began spiraling back to earth. Instantly, she turned and dove, extending her feet, clutching at the fish. When she straightened out her flight path, I could see the fish pointed nose-forward now, its tail waving back and forth behind it, as though it were swimming upstream.

With binoculars, we watched the osprey fly to a huge stack of twigs and sticks at the top of a large evergreen. She called to her hatchlings as she flew, and even at a far distance I could make out the high-pitched whistles of her babies. No longer downy white balls of fluff, the young ospreys lurked at the edge of the nest like a set of determined vultures. Their wings were oversized for their bodies, and they dragged them around like heavy coats.

Beneath the flying fish, mergansers and goldeneyes swam in small groups, dipping their heads and bodies under water, then flapping boisterously, their tails wagging like puppies'. "Like water off a duck," the saying goes, and it is true. Drops flew off them like beads of mercury, leaving them dry and shiny and — judging by their excited quacking — thoroughly refreshed.

In winter I had visited this site many times, but in the cold season the place is not such a panorama of activity and motion. Winter energy is not about circulation. It has its pulse, but it is a slow, muffled one. Swift motion is the pennant of summer, the energy it takes to grow up and grow strong.

Three years ago, I spent half a week alone at the edge of this river, outfitted with nothing but a sleeping bag, one bottle of water, and a small tarp. During my days alone, I sat on the river's edge and watched the activity of ducks, eagles, deer, beavers, and otters.

The play of the otters, the flapping of the ducks, the bellows action of young osprey wings testing out the air — those summer days and nights on the riverbank, everything seemed to be in motion. During the day, I came to believe that summer — the literal and symbolic season of growing and maturing — is about action. But then at night, when my eyes were blinded by the velvet dark of the new moon, my ears alone told me another truth about the growing time.

From the moment of late sunset, until the eastern

sky showed its first delicate band of saffron on the horizon, nights on the river were attended, even summarized, by the sound of water, the circulatory system of the earth. Not just the sound of flowing water, which was ceaseless and hypnotic, but also the intimate sounds of creatures in relationship with water. In the dark, when there is no moon, the river song magnifies itself. I remembered the soft *ploosh* of lake pelicans landing at night on the water to fish, the hollow popping noises of the fish rising for insects, the staccato splashing of a beaver's tail, and the sound of something big swimming across the water with powerful, cadenced strokes.

As the hours passed in the deep dark, I recognized an intimate, subtle pulse thrumming beneath all the animal and night sounds. Without the distraction of sight, I found under all the activity and motion something like the measured tempo of a long-forgotten dance. By morning, I had been given a gift that I would never forget, and it is this: Action without a rhythm or pulse beneath it is not growth. It is just action. A dance without a tempo is just feet roaming around a floor. When a heart begins pulsing erratically, life is at risk.

Sinking my paddle into the water now, I matched strokes with my friend, and our canoe pierced the water and settled into a swift forward glide. We both knew instinctively when we had hit our stride, and the canoe knew it, too. Around us, ducks hurried away with their orange feet whirling like tiny paddle wheels. Lake pelicans swam in small groups, their elegant heads moving forward and back, forward and back, in precise synchrony.

All around me and through me was movement underpinned by rhythm — the dual lesson of the growing season, neither action nor cadence complete without the other. I sank into the steady stride of paddling, my arm muscles and elbows giving me feedback about the pace, telling me how to adjust the measure of my stroke. Some dreams never take root, for all our earnest activity. Instinctively, I have felt a sense of never finding my stride, my flow, when certain projects fell apart before their maturity. And there have been times when my own inner growth has been stymied by an inner sense of chaos and lost rhythm.

My doctor checks my wrist for a series of pulses whenever I go to him for a checkup — a diagnostic tool of Chinese medicine. In a healing-touch class, I learned to feel for several different pulses at the top of the head. At a solstice gathering in the canyon, Alan, a song keeper and drum maker, told us to keep the huge drum beating all night to the heartbeat of the earth. When we asked him what that rhythm was, he told us, "Listen. You'll feel it."

Summer

Our bodies flow with rivers of plasma and salt water set to the meter of a beating heart. Nature, too, has her own circulation system of waters, and her heart is the rhythm of the seasons, constricting the waters in winter, releasing them with a gush in summer. Behind every living thing is a steady, comforting, driving pulse. Behind every dream is a rhythm. Listen. You'll feel it.

ON DECAY AND HEALING

The Strange Comfort of Remains

God is life in abundance wherever life is found, but not for all in every season.

— DANIEL QUINN, *THE TALES OF ADAM*

ONE OF THE FIRST HOT MORNINGS of the summer blazed outside my window. From my bed, I could see the tip of the mountain poking her nose up from the range of foothills like a barnacle-studded spy hopping whale. I hadn't slept worth beans, having retired the night before at about three a.m. to toss among the blankets for another hour or so before I finally dozed off.

Why Buffalo Dance

As a bunch of crows began a raucous chorus outside my tiny balcony, the phone rang, and I reached for it with webs of sleep still swirling around my head. By the time I hung up the phone an hour later, a large, painful serving of emotionally charged life scramble had been slung onto my plate. My hands were shaking, and the sun hadn't even completed its morning salutations.

I pulled on an old shirt and shorts, slipped into a pair of dirty tennis shoes, and called the dogs. I'd been walking them toward evening, when the sun slants golden across the alfalfa fields and the glare is less intense. They bumped into each other and into me with confusion and joy when I hollered, "Walks?" Throwing open the door with more force than was called for, I charged out, my feet stomping up dust clouds in the dry dirt, my breath racing.

I ran headlong with the dogs into the calf-high alfalfa plants green as ripe limes. Out of the tight, suffocating confines of the house, there would be a place for me to set aside the congealing mass of shock and betrayal that had oozed into my hands from the phone receiver. Outdoors, I could find a stabilizing island of peace while I processed words, feelings, and tides of hot, throbbing hurt. There is a place inside each of us that longs for the comfort and soothing of a Great Mother when distress assaults us and we can't find our bearings.

This was the mother I was racing across the pastures to find. Countless times, nature has been this mother to me.

Altitude finally caught up with me, and, slowing down, I noticed for the first time that the alfalfa had begun to blossom. If I sat quietly with the tiny, tender purple sprouts of color, would their beauty and sweetness seep into me? *Is it you?* I asked. *Do you have some peace for me?* But the buds did not speak to my heart, so I continued on. A warm breeze blew from the south, bending the heads of the alfalfa stalks and the taller grasses that waved above it. The dogs raised their noses, and Strongheart's cheeks puffed in and out as he tasted the air. I asked the wind if it had a message of comfort for me. My hair blew into my mouth, and the breeze spoke only to the dogs and the fields, so I kept walking, feeling even glummer as I shuffled along. I was willing nature to give me a *Yes*, and she was answering, *No*. When I took notice of my hands, I found them clenched hard.

At an abrupt dip in the pasture near a north-running irrigation ditch, I slowed down to keep from tripping. Right there, at the toe of my tennis shoe, rested the bizarre message of "comfort" the Great Mother had called me to — a message as unsettling and unexpected as my telephone call.

Behind me stretched a path through the field as

straight as the flight of a crow from my house to this ... pile of mess in front of me. It was an animal, or what was left of an animal. There were feet and clumps of fur scattered like brown and bloodied cotton balls. There was stench and bugs who squiggled and roiled. My stomach instinctively turned over. Ants marched up to the death pile in superhighways, coming from all the sacred directions. Flies feasted on two blue, clouded eyeballs. One was still in the creature's skull. The other lay on the ground, trailing fleshy attachments like jelly-fish tentacles. Before I could stop him, Strongheart grabbed that one and gobbled it down, ants, dirt, and all.

In direct opposition to the scene in front of me, my body vibrated suddenly to an oddly felt sense of reso-nance. For the first time since I'd left the house, I felt like I was in my own skin again. What I had stumbled upon was not comforting in the way I wanted to be com-forted, yet I knew that I was welcomed to this particular place in a way I had not been welcomed by the blossoms nor the breeze.

I growled at the dogs to back off and sunk down in the dirt as close as my nose would let me to this confused jumble of stuff that was once a life. In my heart's ears, I could hear the grunts and cries that surrounded this place not so many hours ago. It is not all sweet-smelling, this magic we call a life. It is not pretty all the time. There are some things we cannot make pretty even though we imagine we can. And there are certain processes that we will betray if we attempt to make them pretty.

Beetles scuttled around like crabs, their feet making clicking sounds over the decomposing flesh. This spot would become even fouler before the bones and fur finally melted like honey down into the soil. No perfume here, not for a long time. And it came to me swiftly, an instant knowing that this rot would take its own time to sweeten. If I tried to hurry the process — carry this mess away in a bag, bury it, spread lime over it, burn it — I would do a fine job of keeping the natural elixir of healing from returning to this place.

I stretched my legs out, and my toe scraped across a line of ants and sent them running in circles. I had been searching for my own idea of peace and solace when I set out from the cabin, thinking it would look like flowers and soft breezes — my own metaphor for welcoming, comforting arms. But the Great Mother knows better than us what we need for healing. Sometimes, what is needed is some decomposition, some dismembering of the way things were before a new, fresh form can arise. Such processes take time, and the time is often not pretty.

Concerning the phone call, there would be no immediate resolution or peace or sweetness, this ground was telling me. But there would be new growth arising down the line, for the phone callers and for me. This lost creature and I would both sweeten together in our own time into a new ground of being. No need to banish the flies for now. Nature loves her processes, rotten or whole, sweet or stinking.

I sent a prayer for whomever this was here on the ground, a humble prayer. She and I were sisters that day, and she was most certainly a fallen relative. I prayed, too, that I would give myself the time and the compassion necessary to let the dismemberment begin and the renewal take root. Strongheart snatched up a delicate cloven hoof still attached to four inches of slender ankle and followed me back home, dancing with joy.

ON CHOICE AND DISCERNMENT

Bear Dreaming Big

The balance of nature decrees that a super-abundance of dreams is paid for by a growing potential for nightmares.

— PETER USTINOV

"BEARS! OHMYGOSH...IT'S GRIZZLIES! Four of them!" When I headed out on a drive over the continental divide with my friend that summer afternoon, I never expected to see grizzly bears. In all my years in the Rockies, I'd never had an encounter with the great bruin. This day would make up for it. I gaped out the window of the truck at not just one bear but a huge sow with three cubs, all galloping along the edge of the highway.

Why Buffalo Dance

The meadow in front of the trees was lush with summer grass and flowers: paintbrush, lupine, and larkspur splashing big dots of color on a vast canvas of green that stretched away from both sides of the road. It was a perfect spot for a gathering of cow elk, so when the animals dashed out of the trees and across the meadow, headed our way, my brain played a trick on me, and I continued to see them as elk until they suddenly morphed in front of my eyes.

The slender limbs of my "elk" turned thick and bowlegged as I struggled to find correspondence between my assumptions and the reality of the creatures barreling toward us. It was their locomotion that brought the truth home to me, the rolling, rippling motion of their loose, shaggy fur as they galloped downhill. Swerving suddenly off to the left, the bears loped in a loose line, with mom leading. From the side, I could see her corded leg muscles bulge beneath her fur, muscles that I traced all the way up to where they culminated in a great hump above her shoulders. Grizzlies!

As the truck slowed down to a stop, I took in the fullness of what I was seeing. Three cubs, lean as greyhounds, charged after their mother and darted across the highway toward the flat, brushless creek curving its way through the meadowland. They looked nothing like black bear cubs, who seem to retain their rounded cuddliness for months. These youngsters looked more like dogs, or large apes, or hunched-shouldered high-school football players with fur capes thrown over their backs.

I bolted out of the truck and raced toward the back to watch the family slow to a lumbering trot as they approached the creek, probably about a hundred yards away. In the round lenses of my binoculars, they were framed with sunlight tipping their long fur. At the creek's edge, the sow stopped with her back to me and sniffed the wind. I was too excited to notice which way it was blowing, or if it was blowing at all. The whole family reunited in the creek and dipped their heads to drink. When they raised their heads one at a time, streams of silver ran down their chins. Behind me, my friend clicked off a series of pictures.

The sow seemed restless, perhaps because of her exposure, and she shuffled off in a trot toward the trees in the far distance. Behind her tagged her conga line of children. In all, they looked like a train: that big, that strong, that powerful. Even when they became just dots in my vision, I could imagine the sound of a steam engine whistle from far off punctuating their journey.

Returning to my surroundings, I saw the breeze tousling the heads of grasses, tilting the flowers. The sky was an arch the color of mountain bluebirds, and cumulus clouds loped by in families of their own. I hoped the bears were as happy to be alive at that moment as I was. Life must have been kind to the cubs these last few months since winter. If it hadn't, the sow would not still have all three of them.

I wondered if the mother bear registered anything akin to human surprise when she awoke in April to discover just how big she had dreamed. Three bouncing babies! How crowded that den must have been! The sow had undertaken three huge summer projects all at once. Success with all three was not entirely in her hands. Not by any means. The season would have to collude with her and provide the food and the good fortune needed to keep her cubs growing and safe. A sow can only do so much on her own. Would her babies steer clear of the threat of raging rivers, illness, injury, fierce weather, cars, humans, and other bears? Would she have the strength and the good health to care for them, to nurse them, to survive so they would survive?

Growing a dream to fulfillment requires consent from the world in many, many arenas. When I was younger, like the bear I would take on many summer projects, dreams that had sprouted like saplings in the spring. I seemed to have energy enough for all of them, but even with abundant energy and intention, I found it was never just my own will that made my dreams mature. In fact, all my greatest successes seemed to come out of the blue. Something was colluding with me in a way I could not begin to fathom. We call events like these "luck," but I think something far greater and more mysterious than luck is at work.

In my autumn years, I choose my summer projects and passions carefully. What can I honestly take on? What can I truly feed to fruition? I could not raise three cubs these days, no matter how much consent the world offered me. Sometimes our dreams are not meant to grow, and outside forces make sure of that. Sometimes, though, we are the force that kills our dream with our own grandiosity, with our belief that we can take on more than our bodies and minds can handle gracefully.

The rains have been good, and the wild berry crop will be abundant. The sow looked round and sleek and strong, even with three hungry mouths nursing from her. She looked to me to be ready for a summer of dreaming big, and it seemed that the summer was prepared to dream big right along with her. Some years it is like that, and some years... well, there are always other summers.

One cub, I whisper to myself as I step back into the truck. *One sturdy cub — two at the most. That's big enough dreaming for me this year.*

ON UNITY
Sundance

Miracles seem to rest, not so much upon faces or voices or healing power coming suddenly near to us from far off, but upon our perceptions being made finer so that for a moment our eyes can see and our ears can hear that which is about us always.

— WILLA CATHER

IN THE LAST WEEK OF JULY, on a morning before daylight, Dave and Teresa picked me up, stashed my gear in the back of the car, and off we drove to the high meadows of Colorado to take part in a Native American Sundance ceremony. It would be my fourth year as a dancer, David's twelfth, and Teresa's first. Originally a tradition of the Lakota people, Sundance is a very old, sacred ritual of sacrifice, prayer, and thanksgiving. The four-day ceremonial dance was outlawed by the American government for many years because of the scarifying element of the dance, which is difficult to watch and not easy to understand if you are not part of the tradition. Now legalized, Sundances are again being held throughout the country, in locations mostly kept secret.

Sundance is a commitment to dance for four summers. It is a grueling ceremony in which dancers are housed away from their families and friends for four days and nights. During that time, the dancers neither eat nor drink. From sunrise to sunset, the Sundance chief leads them in dance patterns around a sacred tree that has been cut, carried, and raised up in a large dance circle in full exposure to the sun. For four days, the dancers shuffle and pray, many taking part in the piercing rituals, some hanging buffalo skulls from the skin of their backs, some tying themselves to the sacred tree with ropes attached to pegs pushed through the flesh of their pectorals. As the drumbeats crest in tempo, the dancers rip themselves free in a symbolic gesture of bringing to the Creator the only true gift they have to bring: themselves, their flesh and blood.

Families and supporters — sometimes several hundred — camp around the dance circle and stand in vigil for the dancers, who are dancing and praying not for themselves but for the good of all. Why and how I chose to participate in the ceremony is a story for another time. This summer memory is about the dance itself and about what it is like to step away from one culture's view of the natural world into something entirely different — even if only for a few days.

How would it be if you lived in a world where everyone believed and behaved as if animals and rocks and trees had souls? Stepping out of the car onto Sundance grounds was like stepping through a portal into that cosmology. Each year, from the moment I entered the Sundance camp, everything suddenly seemed alive and sacred. Of course, everything is always alive and sacred, but it is easy to lose that understanding when nothing in the culture around you supports it. For ten days, though, a bunch of people of every color, every age, and every social stratum pulled their motor homes, tents, and sleeping bags together and formed an amoeba-shaped mass of humanity determined to live with a mind-set different from the one each of us was steeped in all the other weeks of the year.

My group of friends made camp on the eastern edge of the amoeba, and I set out a paper plate of "spirit food" — a small serving of whatever we were eating — to welcome the unseen spirits, the bugs, the Colorado wind, and the ground squirrels who looked on curiously and made little chirring noises. Most of the other camps had done the same. Round white and pastel plates were scattered like daisies over the meadows. One year, I watched a particularly enterprising ground squirrel pull an entire plate of goodies down the narrow mouth of his den. Another, not content with food alone, hauled a bright red scarf down his tunnel in the middle of the dance grounds while we dancers watched and cheered.

Sundance camp always feels a bit like Christmas — a magical time touched with a sense of the holy. Over the Christmas holiday, as at Sundance, people smile at each other for no reason, offer help, share gifts and food and song, and gather together for special feasts and rituals. As a child, I used to wonder why we couldn't keep that Christmas magic all year. Now I know that we could, easily, if we chose to. It isn't just natural disasters and holidays that can bring us together. It is us, ourselves, deciding to be with each other in a different way.

How would it be if you could ask for help from the clouds, birds, sun, and soil and know you would be heard? Within the sacred dance grounds, this kind of faith was a reality.

Preparation for the Sundance took days. Arriving at the dance grounds on a Saturday, Dave, Teresa, and I finally stepped into the sacred circle beneath the sacred tree at sunrise on Tuesday morning. All the dancers carried fans made of feathers. The men blew on eagle-bone whistles to give themselves strength and to call in spirit helpers. Under shaded arbors were friends and families singing along with the drummers at the huge ceremonial powwow drum. In a long line, we danced out into the circle, high on adrenalin and — for me at least — fear.

By the end of the first day, adrenalin long gone, each dancer began to sink deeper into another level of interaction with the surroundings. Evening clouds took on fantastical shapes. Smoke appeared from out of nowhere in swirls above the sacred tree. Shooting stars raced like wild horses across the night sky. A dancer would point to the sky and all of us would nod. The men spoke to the bison skulls they would hang from themselves or drag the next day, and asked them for help and strength. I lay flat out on the ground in my dance dress and shawl, cheek pressed to the dirt, and asked the soil to pull the soreness out of me. Teresa dragged herself over to the sacred fire, which would burn nonstop for the duration of the dance, and listened for the voices of the flames and hot coals for guidance and comfort.

By the following evening, I was on hands and knees, crawling between dance rounds. Throughout the night, I could hear men dry heaving in the portable outhouses. Some dancers had collapsed during the rounds and had been carried to the sacred tree. We still had two days to go.

Why Buffalo Dance

During the next forty-eight hours, the forty of us inside the dance circle, men and women alike, were visited by circling hawks, an eagle and a buffalo in the clouds overhead, and a small patter of welcome rain. I had personal visions of animals in my waking and sleeping hours, some of them creatures not likely ever seen on earth. By the grace of forces greater than all of us, each dancer completed the dance that year. When I stepped out of the dance circle and back into the arms of welcoming friends, I knew I had completed the most difficult challenge of my life, and that I had not done it on my own.

Summer is the growing time, and some growth — perhaps all the really profound growth that will ever come to us — comes painfully. I cannot presume to know what Sundance is like for those raised in the tradition. But for me, a white girl born in New York City, Sundance had an uncanny way of bringing me closer to a relationship with the creatures and elements all around me. Separated from the rest of the camp, left to myself to find a way to cope, I was forced by the dance to look outside of human comfort for help. Everyone else in the circle was struggling as I was. While we tried to be there for each other, there was often not much of us left to give away to anyone else.

By the end of the first day, there was nowhere to turn

but to the Creator — dressed in the robes of her creation — for support. The warmth of the sacred fire glowing small and cheerful through the night reflected a strength not felt by any of us dancers. The clouds offered wonderful respite from the sun when they chose to come our way. The animals in visions, in dreams, and alive all around us came with messages and encouragement. The stress of the dance plunged me into a deeper relationship with nature and spirit — what I call "naturespirit" — because there was nowhere else to turn.

For the longest part of human history, it was commonplace to look to natural creation for insight and guidance, but those days are long gone. Denied books, instructions, and human intervention, many of us today would imagine our tool kit for life exhausted. Those of us who do look to naturespirit for help and relationship often look there with the most surficial of gazes, because we have lost our connection with these relatives and must take baby steps to find our way back.

The intense physical and emotional pressure of Sundance plunged me into a deeper connection with the realm of naturespirit. Deep into the visions brought on by dehydration, fasting, and fatigue, I believed in the sustaining powers of nature and spirit because I *had* to. In having to, I then believed because I *knew*. When knowing came, I walked past hope and past the level of my own well-intentioned wishful thinking. Nothing has been the same since. The living soul of nature remains with me, close by, even when I sometimes forget her. For me, this was the greatest unexpected gift from intentional suffering and sacrifice: that I would find deeper partnership and intimacy with nature and mystery.

There are ways to reconnect with nature that are easier, less grueling than Sundance, but some aspects of Sundance remain pertinent to any attempt we make to reenter our natural home. In these times, we rebuild our relationship with animals and naturespirit by ourselves and within the circle of small, like-minded groups. The Sundance family exists wherever people come together and choose to perceive nature as a relative. Whether for a week or for a few hours, the time we spend trying on this sensibility in a group of affirming seekers is cumulative and life changing.

As individuals, we are each tied to our own Sundance tree. This link, whether an imaginal web, a gossamer heart-thread, or a coarse hemp cord, attaches us to naturespirit. Given the invitation, nature will reel us back in. Silent walks in the forest, nights spent watching the moon, time devoted to playing with a dog, and a few days dancing before a sacred tree are all roads linking us to a more inclusive cosmology, in which we count nonhuman relations in our extended families.

Summer

It has been three years since I completed my Sundance vow. Since that time, I have come to believe that, in this summertime of our evolution, humankind is dancing its own sun dance. My prayer is that, clutched in the grip of our cultural and religious hallucinations, our increasing despair and fatigue, and our collective fears, we will turn to naturespirit for help and guidance because we *have* to. I don't believe societies change voluntarily. Change at such a grand level happens because it is forced on us, and it is being forced on us now by a spasming planet and our increasingly destructive and chaotic technology. When we are finally forced by circumstance and ignorance to move beyond hope into knowing that naturespirit is both compass and revelation, then perhaps we will survive the dance. And the late summer of our collective blossoming will bear a harvest the likes of which we haven't seen for thousands of years.

ON INTEGRITY AND PRESENCE

The Holiness of Magpies

Every creature is a word of God and a book about God.

— MEISTER ECKHART

THE NEST SAT like a frizzy brown tetherball in a tree too narrow for me to climb, on limbs too thin for me to negotiate. On the ground sat a big-mouthed baby bird the size of my hand who looked like a glob of pink Silly Putty covered in toothpicks. The youngster's unopened quill feathers were shaded black and white. His eyes were curious and unafraid. When I knelt down by him, he eagerly opened a red mouth the size of a small halved plum and fluttered hopefully.

Overhead, a pair of magpies shrieked and dove. One of them was courageous enough to poke me on top of my head with a hard beak. I knew they would feed their nestling on the ground, and I knew also that the youngster didn't have a chance of survival down there. Come nightfall, he would make a fine appetizer for a passing coyote, skunk, or raccoon, or perhaps he would simply freeze to death by morning.

In my mind, I clicked off all the reasons to leave him there and all the reasons to take him home. First, the reasons to leave him: *Many birds fall out of their nests; it's nature's way. He'll probably die no matter what you do; humans shouldn't interfere. Maybe the parents shoved him out because he's sick. You don't have time for this.*

Then, the reasons to take him: *The poor little guy trusts me; he's hungry. He's not "a" magpie; he's "this" magpie with the plum red mouth and toothpick feathers; and I'm not "a" human, I'm "this" human, who will feel wretched if I leave him here. I'll make time for this.*

In the course of the world, this interaction between one human and one bird would seem to mean nothing, but I've never been much of a believer in "what seems." We inhabit a grand, big planet, and we affect the doings of the planet by our movements in the small, private worlds of our own experience. This smaller world is an intensely personal one bounded at its edges by encounters with things, places, events, and beings that come to represent the larger world to us. If — as the sages and physicists tell us — on some mysterious and confounding level we are all one, then perhaps the good intentions of one human regarding one magpie amount to something.

Under a shower of magpie curses from above, I picked up the nestling and tucked him under my shirt. At home, I found an old woven picnic basket in the garage. It was a bit ratty, and the weaving was broken in many places. In short, it looked just like a magpie nest. I set the nestling inside a cut-down milk container lined with tissues, put the container in the basket, and put the basket on the stove over the warm pilot light.

Since magpies are scavengers and omnivores like us, I had no trouble putting together food for him. As a base, I soaked some dry dog food until it was soggy, added a chopped hard-boiled egg, part of a banana, and we were in business. Then, I cut a plastic straw in half the long way, rounded the end so it looked like a miniature trowel, and scooped up some of the bird glop. When the picnic basket opened, the magpie shoved his pencil neck straight up, flapped his ridiculous-looking little wings, and gaped so that his mouth lay flat open like a spiral notebook. It was an impressive target with a red bull's-eye and shocking orange border.

He made mewing sounds as I dropped the food into his throat and gargling noises while swallowing it. Three times I scooped up a ball of glop for him before he pulled his head back down, shuffled his wings, pooped, and closed his eyes. This would be our hourly routine for several weeks. The picnic basket easily held enough food for the day, a fresh stack of tissues, and a small bottle of water for cleanup. I christened the magpie Amos, and took him just about everywhere with me. Spring wove its way into early summer, and Amos matured.

Along with glossy feathers and a shimmering tail, Amos was growing a distinct personality. Living with magpies is one thing. Living day to day with one magpie is something much different. By midsummertime, Amos had his wings and his freedom. Living away from the busyness and dangers of town, I chose to let Amos come and go as he wanted. He would return to me with a whistle, still liked to eat from a dish at the kitchen counter, and had made peace with the dogs and cat in some silent manner I would never understand. During the long twilight of summer evenings, he would sit outside with me, prancing up and down my arms and snatching up mosquitoes as they landed to feed.

Amos had the stereotypical raucous, flamboyant, strutting magpie persona. But in getting to know him as I did, I discovered a deeper stratum flowing beneath his everyday magpie-ness. There was a quiet and deep intelligence in his black eyes, and a calm, dignified aura about him that became evident the moment he folded his wings and became still. He had an orderly rhythm to his days — times of explosive chattering and flapping interspersed with times of quiet contemplation and preening. Sometimes, I would come upon him sitting on the back fence rail, his eyes closed, practicing the sound and cadence of human speech. He sounded like a monk, then, engaged in something akin to a Gregorian chant.

Sometimes when I took long walks, he would accompany me, riding on my shoulder or flying tree to tree alongside me. He was a good listener and would give you his full attention when you needed to talk, sometimes muttering human-sounding exclamations of encouragement or surprise. And he was affectionate, too, happy to snuggle into your hands and bow his head for a good rub or to preen the hairs on your arms.

In his active moments, he worked hard and kept fully focused on whatever he was doing, whether it was balancing on the back of a cow or taking apart an old splinter of barn wood. Everything seemed important enough to him to require his all, and I thought that if humans could bring such fullness and presence to all tasks, there would be no work that was undignified or menial, and no play that was not noble and important.

As the summer ripened, Amos spent less and less time at the cabin. Eventually, there came the day when he didn't return home to roost under the porch in the evening. He'd been flying with other magpies, and I liked to think they talked him into running away from home. And so I suppose he did, stealing away like some long-ago schoolboy joining up with a traveling circus.

I missed him for a long, long time. I still miss him in the way that one misses the presence of something holy that has come and gone. If *holy* defines a character that evokes special respect or reverence, there was an unadorned holiness to Amos. He was a devoted keeper of the Original Instructions, or Law of Life. In his way, he tutored me in the qualities needed to live a deeply spiritual, deeply integrated life: focus, stillness, play, friendship, love, beauty, routine, joy.

There is sanctity in every wild thing, a presence that reaches out to anoint us with a goodness and wisdom of its own. We live in a world of untamed avatars, some in the guise of creatures we are most likely to dismiss. No matter their form or color, each creature is a magnificent tutorial on living with presence and integrity. Now when a cloud of black-and-white birds descends onto my bird feeders with croaking voices and great commotion, I remember Amos and I am grateful for the holiness of magpies.

ON CLEANSING AND PURITY
Sacred Waters

Many a time have I merely closed my eyes at the end of yet another troublesome day and soaked my bruised psyche in wild water, rivers remembered and rivers imagined. Rivers course through my dreams, rivers cold and fast, rivers well-known and rivers nameless...

— HARRY MIDDLETON

THE RIVER RAN SLOWLY. In the still of early morning, the calm blue waters had become a giant reflecting pond, and they mirrored a cluster of three mountain peaks that leaned together like a trio of good friends sharing a secret. Along the banks of the river, aspens stood in a shimmering cloud of deep-green leaves.

I'd come with a friend and a canoe to my favorite

place on the river. It had an easy launch site, and from there it was simple to maneuver upstream or down. Paddling out on water as smooth and blue as an eye, we left swirling trails of silver ribbon in our wake. It was a glorious morning. Rain from the night before had hung everything with drops of crystal. Leaves, spiderwebs, tree branches — all shot prisms of color when the sun hit them just right.

I love the sound of running water. All winter, ice and snow lock up the streams and ponds, silencing them. I dipped my hand in the river to remind myself of the delights of water in its liquid form and instantly lost the peculiar temptation I'd had to slip in for a swim. The water was freezing. Goosebumps rose up on my arm when my fingers registered the cold.

The canoe rounded a narrow spit of land jutting into the current and slid into a quiet eddy. From the corner of my eye, I caught a movement and turned to see a large cow moose ambling toward the sandy shore about a hundred feet from us. From the willows behind her stepped a tiny, wobbly calf, all ears and nose. Born later in the season than most, the little guy was brand, spanking new. He walked uncertainly toward his mother, picking up one stiltlike leg after another, putting his coin-sized feet down with great care.

The cow turned to watch him, swiveling her huge

ears. Moose don't see well. It seems that the animal's greatest power of perception is in its enormous, bulbous nose. As the calf made his way toward his mother, our canoe floated to a stop about fifty feet away, close enough for me to hear the streams of water that trickled off the cow's whiskered chin when she raised her head after a short drink. Moose have always ignored me when I've approached them on water. In a canoe, I seem to be as threatening to them as an old stump.

The calf had not quite reached his mother's flank when the cow suddenly stepped into the river, fixing her eyes on the opposite bank. With three long, splashing strides, she was afloat, the current taking her in a curved arc toward the far shore.

Her calf hesitated, arching his head back over his stout neck. He made a quiet little sound, like the beep of a muffled car horn, and tentatively put one foot into the water. The cold must have struck him the same way it struck me, and he jumped backward. Then he came forward once again and lowered his nose to the water, rippling the surface with his prehensile lips. His eyes followed the cow, who was getting close to the other shore. He waited a moment or two longer, shifting from one pencil leg to the other. Finally, he stretched his head out and made a small, awkward leap into the water.

I gasped as he sank under the surface, and then

caught my breath again as he rose like a porpoise and began paddling. His feet struck out at the air, flailing, until he finally gathered his legs beneath him and started swimming along the edge of the current. His mother began pacing back and forth along the far bank, and we both watched the small dot of the calf's head, like a turtle's back, struggling against the relentless pull of the river.

For many minutes, he struggled along. To me, it felt like forever before he at last reached the other side. But still his challenges were not over. The bank was cut away, and what was an easy step for his mother was not so easy for the calf. He tried to get his legs up over the edge, but the bank was too high. At last, he thrust his chin over the bank and somehow pulled himself aground, then tottered over to where the cow waited in a patch of wet grass.

For a moment they stood together, still, under dappled light. Tiny insects danced and hovered around them, shimmering in the soft light of morning. The calf gave himself a mighty shake, rippling from his ears to his stumpy tail. Water droplets cascaded off him like a shower of shooting stars. Sunshine touched the tangle of wet curls on his small cup of a head and tipped the edges of his dripping ears with gold. Shivering, he spread his legs for balance.

Summer

The light, the place, the water, the humbling intimacy of the moment all collided together in a rush of warmth that flooded my chest and shifted the scene in front of my eyes. For a moment time stood still, and I was seeing something other than, and more than, a moose calf shivering by the river. Another, ineffable presence had joined us at the water's edge. The brand, spanking new calf was suddenly more than new to my eyes. He was renewed. At the sight of him, I sank into a memory of frigid water and cold air against my own skin. I, too, had once stood shivering and soaked and stunned on the bank of a river.

The event was called a water purification ceremony, a mandatory part of preparation for a Cherokee ceremonial dance, and everyone — dancers, helpers, supporters — was expected to cleanse ritually by submerging seven times in the river. Baptism is a water purification ritual enacted the world over. The word *baptize* derives from a Greek word that loosely means "to dip or bathe," and more precisely means to plunge something entirely into the water so that the water closes over it. Baptism or water purification is simply a cleansing taken to a ceremonial level. As a baby, I was baptized with holy water sprinkled on my head. The Cherokee water purification was far more intense.

After a chilly sunrise, twenty-five of us were escorted

one by one to the edge of the river and invited to wade in. When my time came, I could not believe how cold the water was. I stepped forward into a wet world black with shadow and fierce with current. Helpers on both sides took my hands to steady me so that I would not be swept away. As the water crept up my ankles, a sharp pain began throbbing at the top of my skull. At waist deep, the cold sucked the air completely out of my lungs. Quickly, I plunged head down into the water before I could rethink what I was doing. Seven times, I dunked. By the time I was done, I couldn't think anymore, see anymore, or move anymore. The helpers gently guided me to the shore where I dropped, shuddering and gasping for air.

Someone brought me a towel and a blanket and some hot sage tea, which I could not drink until my teeth stopped chattering. When the last person finished, David, the dance chief, smiled at us and said, "You are cleansed now. All the garbage you've carried is floating off down that river. If you want to chase after it, go on ahead, but you don't have to. You can let it all go."

Now, the current of memory dissipated as I watched the cow moose begin to lick her calf. Only days ago, she had done this for him after his journey down a hot, gushing tunnel that had deposited him on this shore of his life. Now, she wiped the water away yet again, but this time her infant's journey was a cold one. And this time — unlike the involuntary luge ride of his birth — he took it by choice.

The look of them together — soaked, peaceful, their coats steaming — enthralled me. If I could have turned my paddle into a magic wand, I would have waved it over them in blessing. Mother and infant had brought me into the presence of the sacred — a chance cleansing had become baptism simply because of its beauty. I dipped my hand into the river. Nature — the first baptism. Water, her instrument.

The rite of submersion remains an enigma to me that is ancient, wordless, and profound. I don't claim to understand it. And I don't understand the mystery of water, either. Some scientists believe water is not even of this earth, that it all came in showering balls of ice from the cosmos, and I can imagine that. But I do know that, years past, when I recovered from the shock and cold of my ritual encounter with the renewing energies of living water, I felt buoyant, cleansed, and purified. Like the moose calf, I was strengthened in my encounter with water and made fresh again.

Something deep in our souls calls us to dip into water with our hands, our toes, our whole bodies. The contact is not just for bathing. We play in water, float upon water, and long to live in sight of water. Yes, water cleanses us, but the cleansing goes deeper than the skin. Washing my hands in a bowl of warm water, I imagine washing away something haunting me, and it helps. Showers and baths can serve a similar purpose if we set our intentions for a deep ceremonial cleansing.

At any moment in our journey, water offers us an instrument for cleansing ourselves and starting over again. We did not invent baptism; water did.

AUTUMN

Autumn

West Wind, all that you are —
Season of autumn, house of chill black winds, twilight of the
    day, dying fires of sunset.
Dwelling place of the bear, the raven, and the thunderbeings.
Guardian of the adults.
Place of introspection, harvest, and healing.
Time for putting the garden to rest, gathering the last bounty
    of summer,
And taking stock of the harvest.
Cycle of leaves falling, stems turning brittle, and berries shriveling.
Guide us through this season of turning within, collecting
    ourselves, and preparing
For the deep rest of winter.
Help us to accept what our garden has produced, and to let
    go of what was,
And what wasn't.
Walk with us as we grieve, celebrate, reflect.
There will be other summers.
Hear our prayers that what we have gathered will be sufficient
To take us through the dark nights and cold days of winter.
Hear our prayers for healing the wounds of the past seasons.
Open our ears to the rutting songs of the elk and the
    moose,
Our eyes to the clouds of migrating birds, and our hearts to
    stillness.
West Wind, blow through us. Bring us your blessings and your
    wisdom.

ON RELEASE

Dove in Hand

*The hardest part of anything is the beginning, and
the second hardest part is letting go when it's the end.*

— E. FRITZ

I DON'T KNOW WHY I DECIDED to take my shoes off
and wade into the small, seasonal irrigation ditch along
the north side of my cabin. The rocks are slippery at the
end of summer, having had a whole season to grow a
lovely brown slime all over their faces. They extend
a warm invitation for you to fall flat on your face should
you be enticed by their siren call, but the dogs looked

eager for some new adventure and had already trotted ankle-deep into the middle of the stream.

I pulled off my blue loafers and stepped out into the stream, whispering, "Good dogs, good dogs. Let's go, come on…" For balance, I held my arms out like wings, and walked slowly upstream, bending my head this way and that to avoid the tangle of willow limbs weaving a dappled green canopy over the shallow water. In the golden, shifting spots of light puddled like honey drops along the sandy bank, I first saw the mourning dove. My eyes fell on him and stayed there, mental chatter coming on fast: "What's this? Oh, oh…wings stretched out like that. So still. Oh, goodness, he's dead."

But the tiny black jewel of his round eye denied that. It was clear and bright and fixed on me. I told the dogs to go ahead, and splashed awkwardly over to where he lay fully outstretched, his tail feathers soaking in the water. When I lifted him, he never protested, hardly even moved. His body was cold, his chest scarcely rising, and he had that terrible lightness sick birds get when they are close to death. Through the rose-beige feathers of his breast, I could feel his keel bone and little else. The poor fellow was thin as a twig. Too weak to fight, he rested like a potato in my palm and made no protest when I folded his wings against his body and put him inside my shirt.

Autumn

They always seem to come to me to die, these birds I find along roadsides, under windows, or panting rapidly in snowbanks. I used to feel awful about it, wanting to give them back their lives, when all they seemed to ask of me was a safe place to expire. In my cabin, I found a small box, lined it with tissues, and placed the dove inside. His head dropped listlessly to the side. My antique gas stove has a warm pilot light, and I set the dove there while I made up a concoction of raw egg, warm water, and Rescue Remedy. When I poured it down his throat with an eyedropper, he actually rallied his forces and reached forward to chug down another dropperful, then another and another. By the time I turned the lights out and went to bed that night, he had glugged down several more dropperfuls, plus a few gravel-size balls of mushy wheat bread that I rolled up and pushed down his gullet with a toothpick. At least he would not die hungry on my watch.

When the sun came up bright the next morning, I could not have been more surprised to find him still alive, with his head held smartly between his bony shoulders. And the next morning, it was the same, and the next. The dove had graduated by that time from the small cardboard box to a blue plastic cat carrier lined with a towel and scattered leaves and grass. Now, when I reached in to catch him for his daily forced feedings, he fought me off and snorted half of a very indignant *coo...coo*. I told him that if he wanted to avoid my intrusions, he would just have to start eating by himself, and the next morning, he did, moving his head rapidly up and down over a pile of seeds and scratch, like a finger tapping a typewriter key.

On the sixteenth day of his stay with me, I carried the mourning dove in both hands to my backyard, near the place where I had found him. His breast against my palm was smooth and well fleshed. His beak jabbed against my hand in righteous protest. When I opened my hands to the sky, he exploded upward with a flash of feathers and never looked back. Not once. I headed for the house with a grin the size of a pumpkin plastered on my face and a small stab of loneliness in my chest. A part of me had gotten so accustomed to his company that I wanted to keep him longer — maybe even build him his own aviary.

In the few short weeks of the dove's recovery, the first breaths of autumn had blown into the valley. Chokecherry bushes dressed themselves in dusty burgundy and wore their blue berries like strands of pearls. The breeze that lifted the dove away from my hands was crisp as apples, and the grasses beneath my feet had faded from summer green to soft gold. I had watched the dove's spark of existence grow from a dim glimmer to full life and vigor as he moved swiftly and unexpectedly through a season of growth in only a few weeks.

Here, on the border between two seasons, I performed my first autumn task — that of letting go. Summer draped herself like a long veil down the hillsides and away, showing off her successes in fat ears of corn, tight green bales of alfalfa, and blowing seedpods. The crabapples dropped from their branches like ruby jewels onto meadows strewn with grass seeds and dried wild cranberries. As my hands had opened for the dove, summer was busy liberating the season's successes and failures in preparation for the turning-within of autumn. Had the dove not lived, I would still have opened my hands for him, releasing him into the ground instead of the air.

Autumn calls for both rituals of letting go. There is the need to put to rest the projects that did not grow, to place them gently and without regret into the places that lie within us like burnished old chests holding the wealth of all our unlived dreams and hopes. Next comes the ritual of celebrating the dreams that have matured, and celebrating them with great fanfare, before opening our hands to release those dreams, too. Wanting to hold on to the successes, as I so often do, wanting to luxuriate in them and puff out our chests about them and savor them and put just a few more finishing touches on them, we run the risk of making them wither. No matter how beautiful their fall color, trees release their leaves when the season is ended.

Reaching my hands into the dove carrier to toss away the old paper and uneaten seeds, I pulled out three perfect tail feathers the colors of fall. I placed them carefully on my meditation table to remind me of the need to keep opening my hands to autumn.

ON THE HARVEST

Strongheart's Bounty

Thy bounty shines in autumn unconfined
And spreads a common feast for all that live.

— JAMES THOMSON

OUTSIDE, THE YARD WAS AWASH with the colors of
gold and bronze. Inside, Strongheart staggered around
the room like an intoxicated bear. Yesterday, he was
ambling down the dirt road with Arrow dancing at his
side and pulling on his ears. The next morning I found
him weaving around the living room on weak legs,
crashing into furniture. I hurried him outside where

there was less chance for a collision and helped him stumble down the three short stairs to the yard.

We took a long look at each other. My face furrowed into a frown of confusion. Strongheart stood straddle-legged for balance, his tongue hanging like a roll of pink flypaper. In response to my look of concern, he answered with a face full of apology and gave me a big grin, weaving slowly from side to side. He never liked appearing anything other than majestic. Sickness or injury was shameful to him and a source of great embarrassment.

I walked over to his side and he leaned against me in affection. "It's okay. I'll keep you safe," I whispered into his broad face. I had been whispering that vow to him for eight years, and it had not been an easy promise to keep. Strongheart was gigantic and assertive. With shock collars, muzzles, fencing, training, and assorted KEEP OUT signs, I worked diligently to keep Strongheart out of potentially deadly situations. He had bitten some dogs. Had he been smaller, this would have been nothing serious, but Strongheart had a mouth the size of a breadbox. Even a warning nip could leave massive holes.

Worse, he had bitten a few people, too. I knew that, at 160 pounds, he had the capacity to be accidentally deadly. Although his bites were warnings to people who had ignored either the signs or his furious snarling, I lived in a constant state of vigilance. Years before, I had spent two years at sea on a sailboat. At the sound of rain or wind, long after I had returned home to shore, I'd suddenly sit bolt upright and then scurry around the room in panic before I realized I was safe on land. Living with Strongheart was like living at sea. At the sound of the doorbell, a car, or his bark, I would spring to my feet and race into action of some kind. Put him out. Lock the door. Greet the car. Pull someone away from the electric fence before they tried to pet him.

More than once, the question of euthanasia came up. Mostly, the topic was broached by friends who felt I was living with a time bomb. Part of me believed they were right. The world is full of foolish people trying to make the point that they are not afraid of big dogs. And then there are the people who just don't know better. I kept my promise to Strongheart on a day-to-day basis. In truth, I am ashamed to admit there were times when I wished he would die, because the stress of keeping him safe was sometimes more than I thought I could bear. In these moments, anguish and guilt would flood over me and I would remember once again how much I loved him, vowing yet again to keep him safe.

Now, Strongheart stood before me on shaky legs. For a brief moment his look of apology faded and his bottomless, wise eyes met mine and I knew. This was our last autumn together. He would not see winter.

There were X-rays and blood tests for the next few days, and vets poked and prodded him in private places. Throughout all these indignities, Strongheart remained relaxed and accepting. In the end, it was decided that steroids would provide him relief and balance for some amount of time, but that his spinal degeneration would progress rapidly. My promise to keep him safe became a promise to keep him comfortable.

As the days took on the full magnificence of fall, Strongheart rested in the sun on the back deck, sleeping mostly. Steroids bloated his belly and made him pee frequently, quarts at a time. He seemed content but remained embarrassed about his ungainly motion. Any time he moved from one place to another when anyone was watching, he hurried along as if his tail had caught fire. He could not control his legs well, and this rush of speed often sent him headfirst into a table or wall. It was as though he were constantly saying, "Excuse me...excuse me...," with his body, eager to get away from our eyes, humiliated at being less than kingly.

I ached to think he was ashamed in my presence. But as much as my presence embarrassed him, it also comforted him. He looked to me with questioning eyes, smiling when I assured him that all was well, and that we would be fine. For all his size and courage, his debilitation frightened him. Strongheart, like all animals, was in intimate communication with his body, and I knew he understood exactly what was happening to him.

The blackbirds began massing in large flocks, wheeling in the sky like schools of obsidian fish. As the night temperatures dipped low, the hummingbirds left one by one. The ground squirrel colony in my backyard vanished underground for a long sleep. On windy days, gold leaves blew across the yard like tiny tumbleweeds, and houses that had been hidden behind dense screens of willows and aspens were suddenly visible again.

On these glory days of autumn, two very different vignettes were being enacted in my cabin — one vignette mine, and the other my mother's. My mother was stricken with grief when we were told Strongheart would not live long. Often, I would find her on the back porch stroking him and sobbing, "I can't think of how it will be when he's gone." Already, she was mourning his loss.

Grief is a natural and necessary aspect of autumn. It can seem sometimes as though all the world is leaving and everything sweet is ending. The geese wing away with harsh cries. Summer streams go dry; the leaves dance and are all gone one morning after a hard night's wind. But this season offers another energy that can transform the melancholy into bittersweet: our crop is in

— however grand or lean it is for the year, it is time to consider our harvest.

There was a need in me to remain strong and confident for my dog. Strongheart and I had sowed rich fields together for eight years, so while Mom carried the energy of grief for the two of us, I spent my days considering the harvest. Looking back at my years with Strongheart in the new and sobering light of his leaving, new attributes and gifts became apparent in our journey together. I would not have remembered them all had I not intentionally set aside this time to gather in what we had sowed together.

He had been my brave companion on long night walks into dark forests, both literal and metaphorical. To live with him, I'd had to learn to be as strong and confident as he was, so that we could be partners. When I faltered, he would let me know by peeling his lips back in a snarl and revealing a mouthful of white teeth. He taught me about the subtle art of negotiation.

Our harvest was good. We had our weeds, but they were not toxic. We had grown good things together. Considering our harvest gave me the strength to remember the sweetness when the time came to let go.

On a windy August night, Strongheart made his last effort to stand up and fell with a cry onto the living room floor. While Mom wept and stroked his big face, I moved furniture away from him, lit a candle, turned down the lights, and put on soothing music. Then, I gave him a sedative and called Jane, the veterinarian on night call. I wanted him to be sleeping when she arrived. He would have been mortified at his helpless condition in front of someone who was not family.

I stretched out alongside him and pulled his big body close. As he snored, I whispered to him all the great things we had done together, and thanked him over and over again. "You have been the best of dogs. You have taken care of us and loved us all your life. How will we manage without you? How will I manage? Forgive me for all that I wasn't in my days with you." I marveled at the fullness of our lives together, and then poured all that wonder and sorrow out into salt tears when Jane finally arrived and pressed the plunger on the euthanol syringe into his back leg. True to his name, his heart continued to beat for a long time. When it was over, Jane said that he had died nobly. Only later that night in my room did the grief finally find me and double me over until morning.

Strongheart has been gone for many months now, but each day I find a new sustenance in his memory and taste a new flavor to our partnership. I grieve over the times when I was a less-than-perfect companion to him and weep for the empty place his passing has left behind.

He filled up a space far greater than his magnificent white body, and the cabin continues to feel strangely abandoned. But these autumn memories retain a sweetness as well.

Grief is a signature piece of fall, but so is harvest. When I feel my way tentatively into the spot inside that Strongheart used to fill, I stumble upon an unexpected cornucopia of joy, memory, and learning.

It is our harvest that takes us into the long months of winter and sustains us. If we have done our summer work well, the larder will be full enough of good soul food for us to consume and digest when the year's growing time is far behind us. Fall is the season for both grieving and celebrating what is now behind us, balancing ourselves with tears and laughter, melancholy and joy. When the leaves blow and birds wing in great and urgent crowds across the blue autumn sky, the days for planting and weeding are over. We take up our harvest and bring it inside, inside where the arrows of autumn point us.

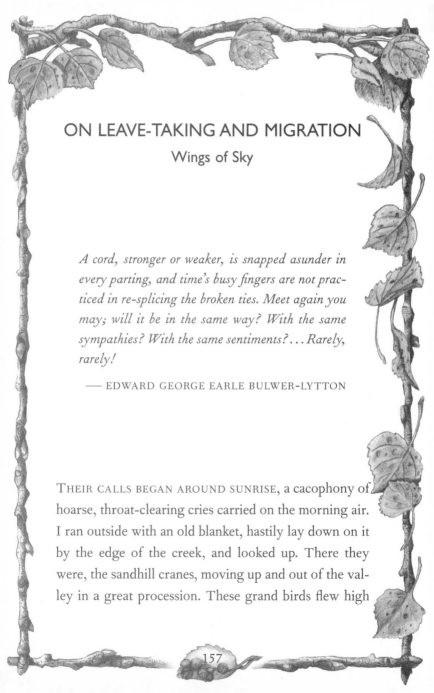

ON LEAVE-TAKING AND MIGRATION
Wings of Sky

A cord, stronger or weaker, is snapped asunder in every parting, and time's busy fingers are not practiced in re-splicing the broken ties. Meet again you may; will it be in the same way? With the same sympathies? With the same sentiments? ... Rarely, rarely!

— EDWARD GEORGE EARLE BULWER-LYTTON

THEIR CALLS BEGAN AROUND SUNRISE, a cacophony of hoarse, throat-clearing cries carried on the morning air. I ran outside with an old blanket, hastily lay down on it by the edge of the creek, and looked up. There they were, the sandhill cranes, moving up and out of the valley in a great procession. These grand birds flew high and in great numbers, like an endless flotilla of faraway steel-gray ships slipping across the heavens.

Through my binoculars, I could see them reaching forward with their long necks fully outstretched and their beaks pointing like slender arrows. If I could have seen the air itself, I would have seen it breaking like a wave over their elegant heads, dancing in spirals down their sleek sides, and slipping with a bubbling of sea foam off the tips of their pointed toes. *Graaaaack...graaaaack*, they called to each other for encouragement as they flew. From their sides sprouted great gray wings the color of a cloudy sky on which they soared, almost motionless, atop the mountain thermals.

For the rest of the day, they would be sailing by, not an hour passing without their calls raining down on me. Although I could not, I wanted to lay and watch them for hours, filling myself up with the mystery of their journey. Deep into the season of migration, flocks of geese and ducks filled the skies day and night, the sound of their wings rustling like silk ball gowns when they flew low overhead. Even birds that would not be leaving gathered up in flocks and surged back and forth across the valley, everyone going somewhere. Yet no flight could compare with the slow, majestic glide of the sandhills.

There is a particular energy in the shifting of each

season to the next, but I don't think any seasonal turning settles as viscerally into any living thing as the movement of summer into autumn. All through the mountains, the animals and birds reflect the coming of the autumn equinox with intense pageantry. It is the season of grand-scale motion, when herds and flocks are on the move, stirred by an agitating whisper that sings of migration. Of all natural rituals, it is the ceremony of migration — of leave-taking — that strikes a deep chord of melancholy within me. Migration is a letting go of yet another kind, far different from release, grief, and the opening of heart and hands to the past. This kind of letting go involves distancing, place changing, and farewells of a different nature.

This year, while the sandhills gathered and the magpies cackled in large flocks around the feeders, I took down my suitcase and a collection of large plastic tubs, setting in motion a migration process of my own. As the cranes winged overhead, I began packing.

I had met my boyfriend the previous winter. For nearly a year, we had gotten to know each other through emails, phone calls, and weekend visits. His home was three hours from mine in the mountains of western Montana. When the relationship deepened, we started talking about ways to spend more time together.

"You could come up and stay a while. We could see

where that goes...if we like each other for more than two days at a time..." Chin up, he peered at me through the bottom of his glasses, through that little spot where you can read newsprint. My schedule was the more flexible one. If we wanted to explore having a relationship beyond weekend stints, it was clear the air currents were blowing from my home to his. I suggested I come to visit for a month.

My boyfriend had lived in his small town for seventeen years. I had spent only three years in mine, yet in those three years I had cultivated the most wonderful friendships I'd experienced in decades and found the sense of community I'd been longing for. So much had blossomed in my three years at my small cabin: a new book, a church community, work, activities, hometown events, strong bonds, and good conversation.

And yet I'd sensed a disquieting restlessness in my limbs developing over the summer as my partner and I juggled our calendars to make way for brief visits. Like geese gathering together in a restive bunch and turning their expectant faces to the fall winds, something within me was gathering up to move. I don't know what it is that pulls the birds onto their migratory flight paths, but what was pulling me dreamily onto mine was an age-old longing for intimacy. I wondered, too, if all those creatures who wander feel a burning, near-equal desire to stay where they are — to root down — as I did.

I packed as lightly as I could for a month's journey, wanting to fly away to Montana and to autumn with as little encumbrance as possible. My car could have held three times the load made up of my spare belongings and Arrow. The morning I left for Montana, the winds were whistling like sirens. A tail wind blew me to the highway and waved me out of town.

At the other end of my ride waited a big house over-flowing with teenage commotion, the largest cat I'd ever seen, and a funny man with a keen wit and intelligent eyes. The skies in Montana are immense, and they were filled that day with flocks of geese, cranes, and starlings and mobs of crows. From every fence post, a hawk watched the wheeling birds overhead. A golden eagle looked down at me from a telephone pole, and farther on, atop the lamppost at an old farmstead, I saw a rare migrating snowy owl perched as still as ice.

Ninety miles out of town, a herd of elk high-stepped across the highway, heads erect and eyes turned toward their wintering grounds. I stepped harder on the gas after they had passed, flying across the asphalt toward my temporary resting ground. Then at the crest of a low hill, I slammed on the brakes at the sight of something large and black lying in a heap on the shoulder. Arrow woke up momentarily as I pulled the car over and ran back to find the body of a freshly killed young raven in the yellow grass by the road.

Juxtaposed against all the autumn journey-makers, he lay terminally still. Even against the stiff winds, not a feather lifted. His open eye gleamed black as jet, and inside it floated the reflection of the moon, still unset. Raven, keeper of magic, had called it down to earth, shrinking it to the size of a tiny pearl and hiding it in his eye. I was shaking from the buzz of my drive and the surge of energy that had spurred me on to this journey. The raven had captured me by his stillness, reminding me suddenly that there are risks inherent in any flight.

Is that the terminus of the melancholy that fills many of us at the sound of geese calling overhead? Inside every creature who journeys is some intuitive knowledge about the risks of wandering far. No matter what the power of that which calls us onward, it cannot forestall the dangers of the passage.

I took a deep breath. Would I find my way back to my friends when my month away was ended? Would I return brokenhearted? More sobering, would I ever go back home again, or would this new place keep me? When you take leave of anything, return is never guaranteed. Still, the desire to move on, move forward, surges up in our throats and sets our feet on fire, and we take leave of what was, sometimes soaring as gracefully as a crane, sometimes flapping wildly like a duck.

I placed my hands on the raven. He was cool and soft and so black that touching him was like touching night. A careening flock of starlings wheeled overhead. The eye of the raven caught them and kept them, and I in turn gathered up the raven and kept him to remind me that life's intrinsic journey — although demanded of us — is never guaranteed, forward or back.

That night, I sat in the bleachers watching the first hometown football game of my life, cheering for my lover's son Alex, in his varsity year. Above the din of two hundred enthusiastic parents, I heard suddenly the croaking call of the sandhills. High over a golden field of floodlights and muddy young men, a flock of cranes like dark stars called down their story of leave-taking, possibility, and peril. In the crowd on the field, I spotted Alex's gold-helmeted head. Come late fall, his team would win state championship under a foggy sky long clear of traveling flocks. Later, he would be making his first migration into the big-town world of college and adulthood. Although I could not know it, nor would I have wanted to know it then, my relationship would be finished by spring, ending in a manner similar to the car-struck raven I had found by the side of the road — so quickly I never saw it coming. Like the sandhills, I would return to my valley to begin a new growing season while my heart revisited winter.

But on that night under the floodlights, Alex played on while his father and I remained encircled under an ancient teaching carried on wings of sky.

ON DREAMING

The Squirrel Who Wakes to Dream

I know now that it is not out of our single souls we dream. We dream anonymously, communally, if each after his fashion. The great soul of which we are all a part may dream through us, in our manner of dreaming, its own secret dreams.

— THOMAS MANN, *THE MAGIC MOUNTAIN*

ON AN AFTERNOON OF BLUE SKIES and mountains etched sharp in the thin air, I traipsed out into a sage field near an abandoned ranch for a 360-degree view of hills, sky, peaks, and an occasional cloud as white as the fleeting bits of autumn snow dusting the mountaintops. In my small backpack, I carried a water bottle and a camera and not much else.

Why Buffalo Dance

Off the corner of a sagging pole corral, mounds of earth rose out of the ground in a haphazard collection of pygmy-size pyramids. Stringing each pyramid to the next was an erratic, faint trail nearly as messy as a snow-shoe track but not nearly as wide. I walked forward to see the large hole at the base of each mound. Badger. In summer, this field pulsed with ground squirrels — chiselers, we call them. By August, the chiselers were fast asleep in deep hibernation. In late autumn when the ground was hard as stone, the badger had come to call, digging out the slumbering squirrels and gobbling them down.

The thought made me cringe, even though my own experience told me the squirrels were so deep in winter torpor that they were not aware of their plight. Years ago, before the era of bubonic plague and hantavirus, I had a tame golden-mantled ground squirrel for a pet. She lived in a large cage on Mom's Formica kitchen counter. Each day, "Goldie" was let out to scamper behind the canisters, over the faucets, and across the toaster to her alternate, napkin-lined hideaway behind the breadbox. Her small pink tongue was busy on those excursions, and we never had so much as a crumb left laying on that countertop. As a treat, we'd let her roam over the dinner table after we'd finished eating, and she loved to eat, hide, and rearrange the leftovers on our dinner plates. We found her antics on the table far more mesmerizing than television, and I have many sweet memories of my family gathered around the table laughing, and of my father pointing at Goldie and giggling so hard that his whole body wiggled. Of course, we never let Goldie do her thing when guests were over. Certainly not. When company came, we pretended the cat never got up on the counters, the dog never licked the plates, and the squirrel never made tracks through the leftover mashed potatoes and peas.

Goldie's first autumn with us arrived, and she celebrated by weaving a huge nest of shredded napkins, tissues, and one dish towel we hadn't rescued from her small jaws fast enough. The creation was quite a feat of construction, filling up nearly all the space in her cage. Perhaps because I was busy starting school again, I didn't notice that I rarely saw her after her nest was complete. In fact, the day came when I realized I didn't see her at all.

Worried, I poked my hand into the depths of her nest and was struck dumb when my fingers closed around what felt like a ball of hard, rubbery clay. From out of the nest, I pulled something that looked like my squirrel but felt all wrong. She was curled up like a pill bug with her tail wrapped up around her nose. There was no rise and fall of her breathing. Her eyes were pressed shut and

I could not open them with my trembling fingers, nor could I bend her legs. She lay in the palm of my hand leaden and paralyzed, and it was my mother who finally told me about hibernation when she found me trying to warm my squirrel over a heating pad under a desklight. To this day, I've never forgotten the feel of my squirrel, dead but not dead, so stiff I think I could have thrown her through an oak door and she wouldn't have felt a thing.

In tunnels beneath the badger mounds, I knew, small squirrels much like Goldie were sleeping, and had been sleeping since August. The ultimate couch potato, chiselers eat until they are as round as tomatoes, then head off to doze until the following April or May. A friend of mine observed, "For chiselers, the world is always summer!"

I took off my pack and sat on it, thinking about another kind of ground squirrel that scientists have studied who wakes up several times in the winter, just enough to dream. The arctic ground squirrel sleeps away eight months of the year, much like the chiseler, and has a hibernating body temperature two or three degrees lower than freezing. As the squirrel settles into this deep torpor, its brain waves slowly disappear, as if it were dead. Then, like all mammal hibernators, the arctic squirrel does something remarkable and mysterious.

About a month into its torpor, it shivers itself back up to normal body temperature for a day or so. During these "warm" times, the squirrel does not wake up. Rather, its brain waves indicate patterns that are the same as those of human beings in REM (rapid eye movement) sleep, or dream sleep.

The squirrels warm themselves this way about a dozen times during the winter months. The metabolic price tag of this warming is steep: to meet it, they spend more than half the calories they stored up over summer. Why do hibernating animals do this? Why waste 50 percent of life's energy to dream?

Aboriginal people, whose creation stories are steeped in images of dreaming and dreamtime, might say that the future is first born in dreams. Some quantum physicists are now theorizing that the aborigines may have been correct. "Each creature dreams of the possibility of the next evolution," writes the physicist Fred Alan Wolf, "so that, for example, the fish dreams of the amphibian, and the amphibian dreams of the bird, and so on.... That ability to sense oneself as something new or altered seems to be vital for survival, for altering the genetic code." We are discovering — again — what the ancient cosmologies intuited all along: that consciousness precedes form, that a dreaming mind precedes and catalyzes matter.

Why Buffalo Dance

We know that nearly all mammals dream. Perhaps every other living creature dreams as well. The building blocks for dreaming are encoded in the simplest of life-forms. So important is the capacity to dream, evolution has never let go of it, no matter what the cost. In their own way, rocks may dream, and the same may be true of water and snow and everything else that has had enough consciousness to find its way into form.

In my early years, I was often called a dreamer. Many people are labeled dreamers, usually in a patronizing tone. Dreamers are differentiated from doers these days, and doing seems to be all the rage. And yet, perhaps it is the dreamers who call down the future and pat it into its first semblance of form. Wouldn't that be the greatest doing of all?

I peeked into the hole in front of me that had been clawed open by the badger, a wide, downward-spiraling pathway of claw marks and small uprooted stones. Beneath my sight, at the place where the excavation stopped, there would have slept a small, curled dreamer. Somewhere close by, a satisfied badger curled up in yet another tunnel, having kicked up a curtain of dirt to cover himself, closed his shining eyes, and settled down to dream. I wondered if the badger had dreamed the squirrels, and the squirrels the grasses, and the grasses the badger.

I sat back on my heels, mystified and awed. *Half the energy of life* spent to dream. Throughout untold ages, the gift of dream has swept along in a thick, passionate current, flowing into the mouths and hearts of all things, enduring because the need to dream endures. Enduring because evolution tells us that the dream is worth the cost, whatever mystery the dream may hold, however it may empower us, delight us, terrify us.

My mind looped like the badger trail back to Goldie, gone now some forty years. I wonder if I woke her up just enough to dream in my clumsy attempts with the heating pad and the lamp. *Dreamer*, I say to myself with reverence for her and all the other squirrels curled into silent circles, for me and my own fragile dreams, and for the badger who swallowed a dream and dreams on.

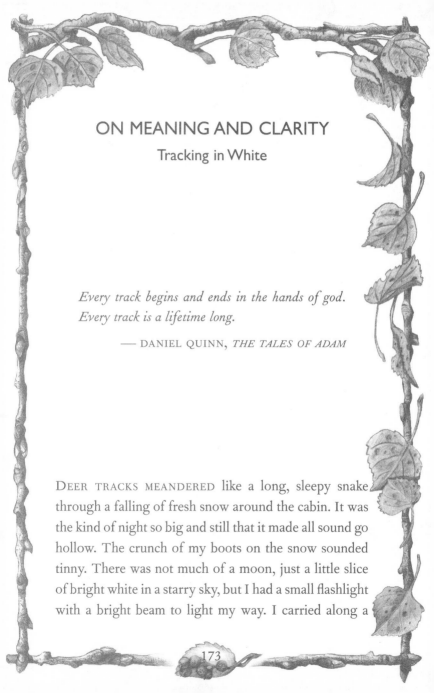

ON MEANING AND CLARITY
Tracking in White

Every track begins and ends in the hands of god.
Every track is a lifetime long.

— DANIEL QUINN, *THE TALES OF ADAM*

DEER TRACKS MEANDERED like a long, sleepy snake through a falling of fresh snow around the cabin. It was the kind of night so big and still that it made all sound go hollow. The crunch of my boots on the snow sounded tinny. There was not much of a moon, just a little slice of bright white in a starry sky, but I had a small flashlight with a bright beam to light my way. I carried along a pocket-size animal-tracking guide and a hanky, because my nose always drips in the cold night air and I didn't need wet blotches all over the pages of my book.

Arrow was delighted to be outside at night and exhibited a special kind of alertness I rarely saw in her during the day. She trotted loose-legged and nose down. Not content to merely sniff the snow, every so often she had to jam her nose down into it, erupting in fits of snorting each time.

At the first temporary snowfalls of the season, I get a full account of whom I share my space with. Spread out on the snow, tracks zigzag, overlap, and crisscross, like crisp numbers on a clean spreadsheet. At night the tracks are especially well defined. If I angle a flashlight beam on them just the right way, it gives them definition and a three-dimensional quality that sunlight would obscure. Besides the clarity, though, the night and my flashlight bring a mysterious quality to the many footprints, as if the indentations were made by invisible spirit animals lurking unseen just ahead, out of reach of my light.

The flashlight beam caught a set of long, cigar-shaped footprints, and I stooped down and cupped my hand at the edge of them, like I do when I'm trying to block the glare from my camera lens. This time, though, I cupped and aimed the light instead of deflecting it. The beam pierced the snow, casting shadows in the cavities of the track. Instantly, the footprints became outlined sharply with gray edges like little walls. Darker impressions were the small, cup-shaped rounds of footpads and the tiny wedge shapes of imprinted toenails.

I never knew I lived with snowshoe hares until I first saw their Twinkie-shaped tracks in the snow, each track splayed out in a gentle V, just like the one in front of me on this night. And certainly, I had no idea of their numbers. This night, the tracks were everywhere, coming from every direction, hopscotching side by side for a stretch and veering off in an abrupt Y.

I followed the hare tracks for a ways, my own boots making holes in the snow, and came to a junction where a much smaller set of prints darted across the hare's tracks, then ran for a few yards making loop-de-loops every which way. The tiny tracks, no bigger than the first joint of my little finger, punctuated the snow with perfect colons a few inches apart, announcing another resident I rarely see during the warm months — a weasel. I shined my light on the depressions so finely etched in the new snow that I could make out even the impossibly small craters of their claws, ringed like half circles of periods around the diminutive basins of their footpads.

Farther down the dry creek bed were the delicate

etchings of squirrel tracks, the exclamation-point trails of mice and voles, and the random inkblot patterns of snow that had fallen from the trees overhead. I bent down to inspect another track of a different sort, a fan across the snow made by the wings of a bird who landed and took off again.

Arrow was completely occupied by the creatures' smells still lingering in their tracks. She followed the tracks by scent. I followed them by sight. I pulled my scarf up over my nose as my flashlight beam caught tiny rainbow flecks of ice crystals in the air. Out into the high pasture, I stumbled across a much larger, bolder replay of a moment not long passed. A great horned owl had thundered into the snow, feet first, wings spread, to snatch a small creature — a vole, I suspect — whose tracks ended there. All that remained of the instant were the splayed, leaflike patterns of the owl's wings, a ragged, irregular hole in the snow, and a few tiny blood drops.

Cheeks numb, I turned and headed back to the cabin, Arrow out ahead of me shining like liquid silver in the spare moon glow. Her footprints ran like ski lines toward the house. Even without the flashlight, I could see the tracks I'd made that evening, slightly toed-out and meandering like a lazy line of surf.

These tracks had followed me every day of my life,

charting my own course, my own map. Someday, like the vole's track, they would vanish, hopefully in a brilliant burst of rushing wind, with a great clutching of sky claws whisking me away somewhere. Meanwhile, I looked back on them, aware that my tracks are so much more exact, defined, clear-cut in snow. I could see so clearly where I'd come from.

Unlike in the summer months, when the lushness and tangle of life can easily hide where we've been, the purity of the cold times outlines the journey in a remarkable, austere way. Autumn is the time for seeing clearly where one has come from. My prints in the snow are held suspended for a few days where I can see them, until the autumn sunshine melts them away or until the next storm. I have time, especially in the dark nights, to shine a small, penetrating light on my tracks and see the dents, the impressions, the hollows, and to find a deeper intimacy with the one who made them.

The process of looking back and dreaming forward can help guide us to the center, to the introspective energy autumn fosters. Behind us, through the summer, we have left a unique pattern of tracks. In the fall, the time has come to better see where we have been and to reflect on the journey. Did we run helter-skelter through the warm months? Do our tracks show a pattern and a pace? Where did the months take us?

Why Buffalo Dance

At the cabin door, a thin spatter of snow blanketed the welcome mat. Interlaced across the surface were the fragile footprints of deer mice and the emptied hulls of pumpkin seeds I'd scattered earlier in the evening. I took a long, awkward step over the doorjamb to avoid sullying the lovely picture of feet and life, and called Arrow around to the back door.

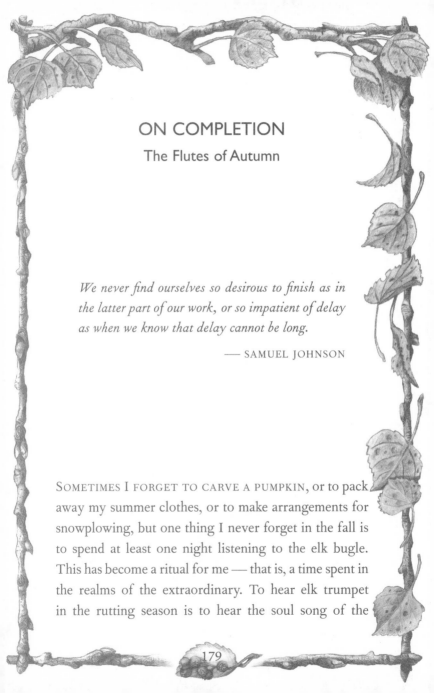

ON COMPLETION
The Flutes of Autumn

We never find ourselves so desirous to finish as in the latter part of our work, or so impatient of delay as when we know that delay cannot be long.

— SAMUEL JOHNSON

SOMETIMES I FORGET TO CARVE A PUMPKIN, or to pack away my summer clothes, or to make arrangements for snowplowing, but one thing I never forget in the fall is to spend at least one night listening to the elk bugle. This has become a ritual for me — that is, a time spent in the realms of the extraordinary. To hear elk trumpet in the rutting season is to hear the soul song of the mountains bellowed through the windpipe of a wild creature.

This fall, I had waited until late September to hear them. There is an abandoned ranch in the park where a huge expanse of grass spreads out like a lake before a colony of dilapidated log buildings and sheds. Ringing the meadow is a circle of mountains. Beneath the mountains is a surround of evergreens crisscrossed by horse paths and game trails. Into those trees is where I always go to hear the elk, usually just at sunset. I take along a water bottle, a blanket, and a warm jacket. It gets bitter cold there if the evening wind blows up.

On this particular September afternoon, I had brought my mother along to share the elk music with me. At eighty-three, she is more surefooted than I am on the dirt path into the forest. We sat on a couple of old plaid throws beneath the same tree I always sit under. In front of us rested a large boulder and a fat fallen log that offered us an elk blind of sorts. Plenty of daylight still remained.

Usually, the elk are bugling before we ever get into the trees, but this evening we heard nothing for a long time. Perhaps we had come too early. Then, finally, it came: a prolonged guttural groan, like wind forced through a culvert, followed by an eerie, high-pitched wailing that finally drifted off into silence. My mom and I looked at each other with mixed expressions of delight and surprise. It is always like that — the surprise that comes with hearing them for the first time in a year. Surprise! It is autumn again! Surprise! Passion is alive and well under the scarlet mountain ash trees. Surprise, too, because the sound is so otherworldly, so unusual, that it is impossible not to be startled by it. When I first heard the elk call, I thought it sounded like dinosaurs bellowing.

I've initiated many newcomers to the ritual of the elk. Invariably, they reflect back to me that same stunned awe that is still with me after a decade of listening to the bulls' symphony. The most common exclamation is a whispered "Oh...my...god" accompanied by an open mouth and wide, wide eyes.

As Mom and I sat quietly, other bulls took up the call, their voices unique, yet all following a similar pattern of guttural grunt and high, thin whistle. As the evening wore on, some would break the call in half and just grunt over and over again. Some would whistle like flute players, forgetting the bass vibrato altogether.

After what seemed like a prolonged bout of elk silence, I decided to creep over to the boulder and look across the meadow while there was still enough light to do it. As my head poked cautiously over the tip of the rock, I found myself face-to-behind with a huge bull grazing quietly only twenty feet away. Out beyond him stretched a line of others. I started counting. Fifteen bulls were dotting the meadow, all of them heavily antlered.

I crawled quickly back to Mom and motioned toward the boulder. She crawled after me, catching her white ponytail in a sage bush. The bulls moved slowly across the meadow, grazing, eyeing each other. Their backs were the color of tawny stone, their legs the shade of wet soil. From their heads sprouted bark-colored branches. They were walking versions of the mountains behind them, the same in color and texture. When one of them raised his head to bugle, the sound seemed to come up from the very ground itself.

When the sun fell entirely and stars lit up the mountains, the elk began to spar. We could no longer see them, but we could hear the sound of antlers clacking and hooves pounding through the grass. For the bulls, everything they had accumulated over the summer — health, vigor, muscle, horn, boldness — was on the line. They would either triumph over competing bulls and find cow elk to mate with, or they would head into winter with their seed unsown.

I listened to them with longing as I always did. The primordial notes of their cry were to me the uncensored sounds of creation and passion. I wondered if any inspired endeavor in my life, if put to sound, could make a music so bold, so wild, and so free.

Autumn

Through the last weeks of elk courtship, the mountains announced the coming of the still, white, silent days ahead. The elk sang the song of summer's last campaign — a crusade of purpose and pride. Everywhere, autumn was packing up, putting away, clearing the palette, reminding us all to do the same after we'd voiced our last, satisfied hurrah and cast over the ground our very last seeds.

In the starry darkness, crisp leaves rustled on the aspens. The night sky had become bigger, the stars closer, as autumn lengthened. Soon the fall winds would turn to gales, the elk would move off these mating grounds, and the land would be covered once more in the freezing white quilts of winter. In these last moments of autumn, creative urgency erupts through life like a geyser. With so little time left to finish up the growth begun in the previous seasons, the tempo peaks, the sound of the season ascends into one last crescendo. It is the last chance — the last chance of the year. *Brrruuuugggh — a-wieeeee!* The bull roars impatiently into the night, his feet stamping like a metronome clicking out the pulse of beating wings and cascading leaves.

Before the north winds engulf us, there is yet this last moment to dare, to hasten, to complete just one more important thing. Is there one dream left in you to finalize with a flurry of passionate zeal before the snows come? Don't wait. Do it now. Winter is coming.

ACKNOWLEDGMENTS

I HAVE WANTED TO WRITE this book for a long time. It is actually the book I had in mind to write when I sat down to pen *Animals as Teachers and Healers*, but somehow it didn't quite happen like that. Here it is at last, and here are just a few of the people I want to thank for guiding me, commenting on my work, reading drafts, and holding my hand and my heart steady along the way:

Thank you, first, to my publisher, New World Library, and to my wonderful editor, Georgia Hughes. For your continuing willingness to stay on the phone and listen while I ramble and hack my way through issues of format, content, and vision, Georgia, I bow to you.

Thank you to my valley friends and mentors: Carol Taylor, Lee Fuller, and Hally Loe — all women with spunk, intelligence, rare depth, and splendid humor. You have made this place home to me, and have become precious family to me, in three short years.

Thank you to the land and the animals and all the earth's relatives for collectively remaining my compass and my anchor.

Thank you, Strongheart, my big white ghost dog, for eight incomparable years. You walked most of the trails of this book with me and showed me where to look and how to ask. You are missed.

And finally, a humble and heartfelt thank-you to my readers. You have kept my back straight and my feet moving forward. I wouldn't do this without you.

ABOUT THE AUTHOR

SUSAN CHERNAK MCELROY is a storyteller and teacher. She has written numerous books, including the best-selling classic *Animals as Teachers and Healers*, and has been featured in a host of anthologies that explore the relationships between humans, animals, and the wild. She lives in Teton Valley, Idaho. Her website is www.susanchernakmcelroy.com.